POPULATION AND OVERCROWDING

MASON CREST
PHILADELPHIA

AFRICA: PROGRESS AND PROBLEMS

POPULATION AND OVERCROWDING

Tunde Obadina

Mason Crest
Philadelphia

Frontispiece: View of Nairobi, Kenya, one of the largest cities in Africa. It is home to more than 3.5 million people.

Mason Crest
450 Parkway Drive, Suite D
Broomall, PA 19008
www.masoncrest.com

© 2014 by Mason Crest, an imprint of National Highlights, Inc.

Printed and bound in the United States of America.

CPSIA Compliance Information: Batch #APP2013. For further information, contact Mason Crest at 1-866-MCP-Book

First printing
1 3 5 7 9 8 6 4 2

Library of Congress Cataloging-in-Publication Data

Obadina, Tunde.
  Population and overcrowding / Tunde Obadina.
    p. cm. — (Africa: progress and problems)
  Includes bibliographical references and index.
  ISBN 978-1-4222-2945-3 (hc)
  ISBN 978-1-4222-8890-0 (ebook)
  1. Africa—Population—Juvenile literature. 2. Overpopulation—Juvenile litera-
  ture. 3. Rural-urban migration—Africa—Juvenile literature. 4. Cities and
  towns—Africa—Growth—Juvenile literature. 5. Africa—Social conditions—
  Juvenile literature. 6. Africa—Economic conditions—Juvenile literature. I. Title.
  II. Series: Africa, progress & problems.
  HB3661.A3O23 2013
  363.91096—dc23
                                    2013013034

Africa: Progress and Problems series ISBN: 978-1-4222-2934-7

Table of Contents

AFRICA: PROGRESS AND PROBLEMS

THE PROMISE OF TODAY'S AFRICA

by Robert I. Rotberg

Today's Africa is a mosaic of effective democracy and desperate despotism, immense wealth and abysmal poverty, conscious modernity and mired traditionalism, bitter conflict and vast arenas of peace, and enormous promise and abiding failure. Generalizations are more difficult to apply to Africa or Africans than elsewhere. The continent, especially the sub-Saharan two-thirds of its immense landmass, presents enormous physical, political, and human variety. From snow-capped peaks to intricate patches of remaining jungle, from desolate deserts to the greatest rivers, and from the highest coastal sand dunes anywhere to teeming urban conglomerations, Africa must be appreciated from myriad perspectives. Likewise, its peoples come in every shape and size, govern themselves in several complicated manners, worship a host of indigenous and imported gods, and speak thousands of original and five or six derivative common languages. To know Africa is to know nuance and complexity.

There are 54 nation-states that belong to the African Union, 49 of which are situated within the sub-Saharan mainland or on its offshore islands. No other continent has so many countries, political divisions, or members of the General Assembly of the United Nations. No other continent encompasses so many distinctively different peoples or spans such geographical disparity. On no other continent have so many innocent civilians lost their lives in intractable civil wars—15 million since 1991 in such places as Algeria, Angola, the Congo, Côte d'Ivoire, Liberia, Sierra Leone, and Sudan. No other continent has so many disparate natural resources (from cadmium, cobalt, and copper to petroleum and zinc) and so little to show for their frenzied exploitation. No other continent has proportionally so many people subsisting (or trying to) on less than $2 a day. But then no other continent has been so beset by HIV/AIDS (30 percent of all adults in southern Africa), by tuberculosis, by malaria (prevalent almost everywhere), and by less well-known scourges such as schistosomiasis (liver fluke), several kinds of filariasis, river blindness, trachoma, and trypanosomiasis (sleeping sickness).

Africa is among the most Christian continents, but it also is home to more Muslims than the Middle East. Apostolic and Pentecostal churches are immensely powerful. So are Sufi brotherhoods. Yet traditional African religions are still influential. So is a belief in spirits and witches (even among Christians and Muslims), in faith healing and in alternative medicine. Polygamy remains popular. So does the practice of female circumcision and other long-standing cultural preferences. Africa cannot be well understood without appreciating how village life still permeates the great cities and how urban pursuits engulf villages. Africa can no longer be considered predominantly rural, agricultural, or wild; more than half of its peoples live in towns and cities.

Political leaders must cater to both worlds, old and new. They and their followers must join the globalized, Internet-

Africa

⊛ National Capital

• Other City

0   500   1000 mi

0   500   1000 km

Azimuthal Equal Area Projection

penetrated world even as they remain rooted appropriately in past modes of behavior, obedient to dictates of family, lineage, tribe, and ethnicity. This duality often results in democracy or at least partially participatory democracy. Equally often it develops into autocracy. Botswana and Mauritius have enduring democratic governments. In Benin, Ghana, Kenya, Lesotho, Malawi, Mali, Mozambique, Namibia, Nigeria, Senegal, South Africa, Tanzania, and Zambia fully democratic pursuits are relatively recent and not yet sustainably implanted. Algeria, Cameroon, Chad, the Central African Republic, Egypt, the Sudan, and Tunisia are authoritarian entities run by strongmen. Zimbabweans and Equatorial Guineans suffer from even more venal rule. Swazis and Moroccans are subject to the real whims of monarchs. Within even this vast sweep of political practice there are still more distinctions. The partial democracies represent a spectrum. So does the manner in which authority is wielded by kings, by generals, and by long-entrenched civilian autocrats.

The democratic countries are by and large better developed and more rapidly growing economically than those ruled by strongmen. In Africa there is an association between the pursuit of good governance and beneficial economic performance. Likewise, the natural resource wealth curse that has afflicted mineral-rich countries such as the Congo and Nigeria has had the opposite effect in well-governed places like Botswana. Nation-states open to global trade have done better than those with closed economies. So have those countries with prudent managements, sensible fiscal arrangements, and modest deficits. Overall, however, the bulk of African countries have suffered in terms of reduced economic growth from the sheer fact of being tropical, beset by disease in an enervating climate where there is an average of one trained physician to every 13,000 persons. Many lose growth prospects, too, because of the absence of navigable rivers, the paucity of ocean and river ports, barely maintained roads, and few and narrow railroads. Moreover, 15 of Africa's countries are landlocked, without comfortable access to relatively inexpensive waterborne transport. Hence, imports and exports for much of Africa are more expensive than elsewhere as they move over formidable distances. Africa is the most underdeveloped continent because of geographical and health constraints that have not yet been overcome, because of ill-considered policies, because of the sheer number of separate nation-states (a colonial legacy), and because of poor governance.

Africa's promise is immense, and far more exciting than its achievements have been since a wave of nationalism and independence in the 1960s liberated nearly every section of the continent. Thus, the next several decades of the 21st century are ones of promise for Africa. The challenges are clear: to alleviate grinding poverty and deliver greater real economic goods to larger proportions of people in each country, and across all countries; to deliver more of the benefits of good governance to more of Africa's peoples; to end the destructive killing fields that run rampant across so much of Africa; to improve educational training and health services; and to roll back the scourges of HIV/AIDS, tuberculosis, and malaria. Every challenge represents an opportunity with concerted and bountiful Western assistance to transform the lives of Africa's vulnerable and resourceful future generations.

1 OVERVIEW

By various measures, Africa—particularly the part of the continent that lies south of the Sahara Desert—is the least developed and most impoverished region of the world. Eighteen of the 20 poorest countries in the world, according to World Bank estimates for 2012, are in sub-Saharan Africa. Nearly half of all people in the region live in extreme poverty, surviving on less than $1 per day. The United Nations Development Program's human development index (HDI)—which takes into account life expectancy, adult literacy and school enrollment rates, and per capita income—paints an equally bleak picture of life in sub-Saharan Africa. Of the 32 countries classified as having low human development according to the HDI criteria, all but 2 are in sub-Saharan Africa. The region also suffers from the highest infant mortality rate: for every 1,000 babies born alive in sub-Saharan Africa, 77 will die before their first birthday, according to World Bank statistics compiled in 2012. That's nearly twice as high as the infant mortality rate for the world as a whole (about 40 deaths per 1,000 live births) and much higher than the region with the second-highest infant mortality rate, South Asia (52 deaths per 1,000 live births).

Africa also has the highest rate of population growth. In July 1950, according to the United Nations Population Division, the continent was home to an estimated 224 million people. By July 2013 that number had risen to more than 1 billion—an increase of more than 300 percent in only seven decades. Africa's population growth during this period far outstripped the rate for the developed world or even for other fast-growing developing regions, such as Asia (163 percent) and Latin America and the Caribbean (211 percent).

In the coming decades, Africa's rate of population growth will continue to exceed that of all other regions. Between now and 2050, according to U.N. Population Division projections, the number of people on the continent will more than double, to about 2 billion. At that time, Africa is expected to be home to more than one in five (21.3 percent) of all people on the globe— up from less than 9 percent in 1950 and 14 percent in 2005. And the vast majority of the continent's people—some 1.7 billion— will be in the impoverished sub-Saharan region.

TOO MANY PEOPLE?

The combination of sub-Saharan Africa's fast-growing population and its extreme poverty has led to the widespread assumption that the region—or at the very least, most of its nations— have too many people for available resources to support. Proponents of this view argue that rapid population growth is putting more and more pressure on Africa's fragile land, contributing to declining agricultural yields and recurring famines in certain countries. Many of Africa's countries, which remain largely reliant on agriculture, cannot feed themselves. In

September 2005 the UN Food and Agriculture Organization (FAO) reported that 24 African countries faced food emergencies.

The needs of Africa's growing population also threaten to outstrip the continent's limited supplies of freshwater. Overall, Africa has only about 9 percent of the world's freshwater—considerably less than its share of global population—though the western and central parts of the continent are better endowed with this vital resource than are the northern, southern, and

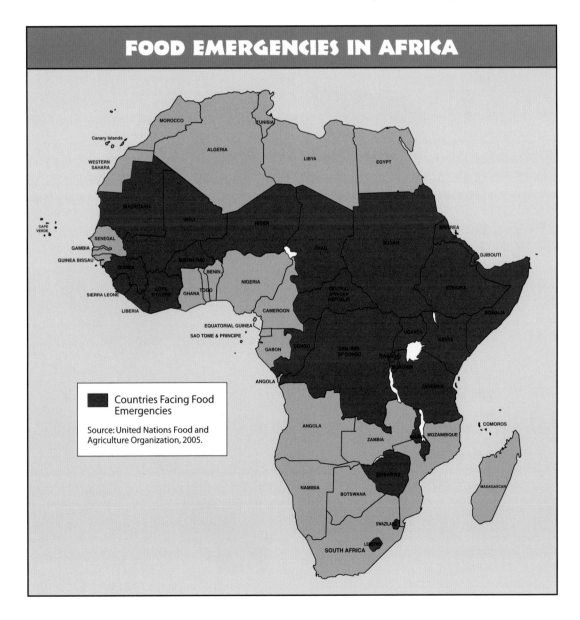

FOOD EMERGENCIES IN AFRICA

■ Countries Facing Food Emergencies

Source: United Nations Food and Agriculture Organization, 2005.

eastern regions. The drier areas of Africa face the prospect of severe water shortages in the decades to come. According to a report by the United Nations Development Program (UNDP), 13 African countries already suffer from water stress (defined as the availability of less than 1,500 cubic meters of water per person per year) or water scarcity (less than 1,000 cubic meters per person per year), and by 2025 another dozen countries will join that number. Combined, these countries will be home to nearly

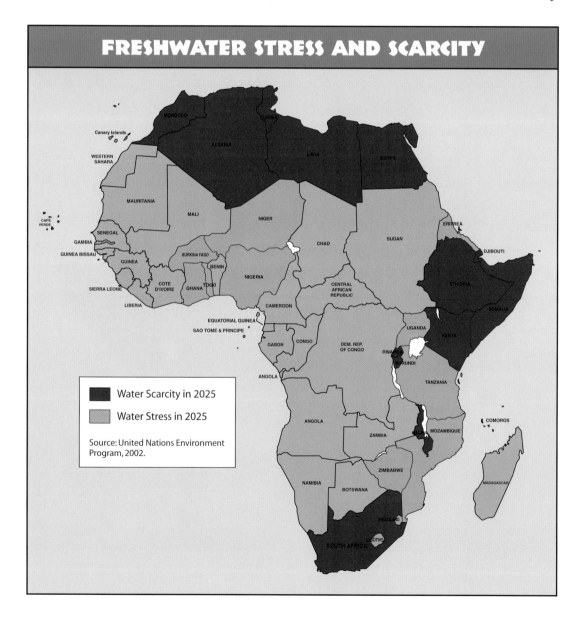

FRESHWATER STRESS AND SCARCITY

Water Scarcity in 2025

Water Stress in 2025

Source: United Nations Environment Program, 2002.

half of Africa's people. The UNDP warned that Africa could witness violent conflicts over water, particularly in areas where rivers and lakes are shared by a number of nations. Such areas include the Nile, Niger, Volta, and Zambezi basins.

High population growth, many observers assert, has seriously impeded the ability of African governments and development agencies to provide adequate social services for the growing numbers of poor people. In turn, the absence of these services, including education and health care, contributes to a cycle of poverty and national underdevelopment.

Another problem believed to be exacerbated by Africa's rapidly growing population is overcrowding in the continent's urban areas. Many African cities have been expanding at a dizzying pace, a trend that has been accompanied by a host of problems. These range from inadequate electricity and sanitation to environmental degradation, high crime rates, and homelessness.

The belief that Africa's predicament is at least partly an overpopulation problem has led various international agencies and aid groups to the conclusion that, if the continent is ever to emerge from underdevelopment, its rate of population growth will have to be slowed. Population trends in a given region are driven by three factors: fertility, mortality, and migration. Reducing mortality rates is a major goal of development; and Africa, like other less developed regions, sends more migrants to the rest of the world than it receives. So when development officials urge African countries to cut their population growth rates, what they are advocating is the reduction of fertility—that is, a decrease in the average number of children born per woman. Family planning programs would have to play a key role in any such effort.

OPPOSING VIEW

Many Africans vehemently reject this prescription, which conflicts with the high value placed on large families in traditional

African societies. In addition, some African nationalists suspect that behind Western population advice lurk racial and political motivations—specifically, the goal of minimizing the proportion (and the influence) of the world's nonwhite peoples. Given the history of European domination and exploitation of other regions—a history that includes the African slave trade and colonialism—this suspicion is perhaps understandable.

Yet resistance to the birth control programs advocated by international donor agencies is by no means limited to Africans holding onto traditional values or to those who suspect Western ulterior motives. Many African leaders—along with a number of economists and development specialists—question the fundamental assumptions of experts who believe Africa needs to slow its rapid population growth in order to emerge from underdevelopment. These people are generally skeptical of population-related explanations for Third World poverty. More specifically, they deny that Africa has more people than its available resources can support. In short, they do not believe that Africa is overpopulated.

At the very least, the belief that Africa is underdeveloped largely because it is overpopulated, and that any path to greater prosperity must include lower population growth, can be characterized as simplistic. Africa overall has fewer people per square mile than highly prosperous Europe or the United States. Moreover, discussion of conditions in Africa as a whole obscures a basic reality: Africa is a vast continent, and among its 54 countries there is great variation in population. For example, sparsely populated Namibia had only about 6.4 people per square mile in 2006, whereas Nigeria had 370, Rwanda 850, and the island nation of Mauritius 1,723.

Second, the continent's impoverished nations include some that are sparsely populated, such as Niger (27 people per square mile) and Somalia (36 people per square mile), and others that are more densely populated, such as Malawi (285 people per square mile) and Burundi (752 people per square mile). Similarly, Africa's more prosperous countries include sparsely populated Namibia, Botswana (7.5 people per square mile), and Libya (8.8 people per square mile), as well as more densely populated South Africa (94 people per square mile) and Mauritius. This indicates that population density alone doesn't determine a nation's prospects for development.

Nor can the predicament of Africa's impoverished nations be explained simply by saying that they have more people than their natural resources and land can sustain. Japan, for example, has about one-sixth the area of the Democratic Republic of the Congo (DRC) but more than twice as many people. Unlike the DRC, which has abundant mineral deposits (including cobalt, copper, petroleum, diamonds, gold, silver, zinc, and uranium), Japan is a resource-poor country. Yet the Japanese people enjoy a standard of living that is vastly greater than that of their counterparts in the DRC. One particularly illuminating measure of this disparity is gross domestic product (GDP) per capita—essentially each citizen's average share of the value created annually by the nation's economy. In 2005 GDP per capita for the DRC was estimated at $700; for Japan the figure stood at $31,500.

Workers dig for copper at a mine in the Democratic Republic of the Congo. Despite a wealth of natural resources, and despite the fact that it is less densely populated than the nations of western Europe, Japan, or the United States, the DRC remains desperately poor—evidence that African poverty cannot be explained simply by asserting that African countries have more people than their available resources can sustain.

STATISTICAL SHORTCOMINGS

It is important to bear in mind certain points when assessing the likely impact of population growth in Africa. First, population projections—even when provided by the most reputable organizations—are not facts. Rather, they are predictions based on assumptions about how a complex set of factors (including fertility rates, mortality rates, and patterns of migration) will play out over a period of time. If the assumptions prove faulty, the projections will be inaccurate. Not surprisingly, the further into the future population projections are extended, the greater the possibility they will be wildly off the mark. This is the case not only because the impact of even a relatively minor variance in predicted and actual birth or death rates can be magnified over the course of several generations, but also because certain events that may have a large effect on population (such as wars and disease epidemics) are unforeseeable.

A further complication, particularly with developing countries, involves the accuracy of current and historical population statistics. Many poor nations have inadequate facilities for collecting and processing data, and sometimes their censuses are tainted by politically motivated manipulation. As a result, it may be impossible to say with confidence how many people live in a country at present, or how many people were living there at given times in the past—essential information for predicting how many people the country will contain at some point in the future.

Nigeria provides a good illustration of the uncertainties of population statistics. In March 2006, as the country conducted its first census in 15 years, estimates of Nigeria's total population varied by as much as 20 percent, ranging between 120 million and 150 million. (The difference of 30 million is greater than the population of the majority of the world's countries.) The official results of the Nigerian census were released in late 2006, but many observers believed the data to be inaccurate, as the March count had been accompanied by confusion, violence, and a boycott by separatists. There were also fears that the numbers would be manipulated—as is widely believed to have occurred during past Nigerian censuses—to advance the interests of specific regions and ethnic groups.

A deeply flawed Nigerian census could have profound implications—and not simply for Nigeria. Africa's most populous country, Nigeria may be home to nearly one in every six people on the continent. Major errors in the base population data for Nigeria would inevitably skew demographic projections for all of Africa.

The example of Japan also helps dispel two other misconceptions about population, overcrowding, and poverty in Africa. First, the fact that a country has more people than its domestic agricultural producers can feed does not necessarily mean that country's citizens will suffer from hunger or malnutrition—Japan, like other prosperous nations such as Switzerland and the Netherlands, relies heavily on food imports. Second, even very high concentrations of people do not necessarily produce overcrowding—if that term is defined as the presence of more people than can be provided a decent standard of living through available resources and basic public services. Tokyo, the Japanese capital, is among the world's most densely populated places, yet its citizens do not lack decent housing, schools, roads, sanitation, or health care. Most visitors would consider the city congested, yet it functions well.

Historical precedents also suggest that rapid population growth such as Africa has recently experienced need not preclude economic development. For example, World Bank statistics indicate that during the period 1980–1990, India—like more than 30 sub-Saharan African countries—had an average annual population growth rate in the 2.0–3.0 percent range. Despite its fast-growing and enormous population—with over a billion people, India's population exceeds that of the entire continent of Africa—the Asian nation has enjoyed more than a decade of robust and sustained economic growth. Since the mid-1990s, India's economy has expanded at an average annual rate of about 7 percent—enough to reduce the proportion of Indians living in poverty by 10 percent.

Nevertheless, it is undeniable that rapid population growth complicates the quest to improve general prosperity. For example, if a nation's economy expanded annually by 7 percent (an excellent rate), that nation's GDP would nearly double in 10 years. But with population increasing annually at 2.5 percent, it

AFRICAN POPULATION DENSITY

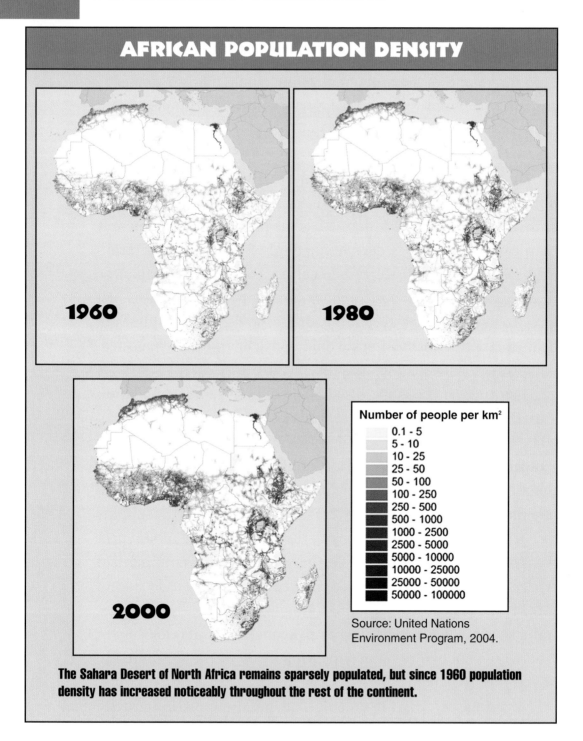

1960

1980

2000

Number of people per km²

0.1 - 5
5 - 10
10 - 25
25 - 50
50 - 100
100 - 250
250 - 500
500 - 1000
1000 - 2500
2500 - 5000
5000 - 10000
10000 - 25000
25000 - 50000
50000 - 100000

Source: United Nations
Environment Program, 2004.

The Sahara Desert of North Africa remains sparsely populated, but since 1960 population density has increased noticeably throughout the rest of the continent.

would take 16 years, not 10, to double GDP per capita (which would be growing at a much more modest rate of 4.5 percent). The faster a country's population increases, the higher the rate of economic growth necessary to improve the material circumstances of the public as a whole. And of course, if population growth exceeds GDP growth, then GDP per capita will decline—meaning essentially that the average citizen becomes poorer.

Africa's predicament is that over the past 50 years, economic growth has barely kept pace with population growth. Thus, its people as a whole are only marginally better off than they were in the middle of the 20th century—whereas people in most other areas of the world have enjoyed substantial material gains.

Will this dismal trend continue? Is population growth crippling African prospects for development, or are other factors more responsible for poverty on the continent? What demographic changes are taking place in Africa today? What will the continent's societies look like in the decades to come? This book will attempt to answer these and other crucial questions.

A BRIEF HISTORY OF POPULATION GROWTH IN AFRICA

Modern scholars can offer only rough estimates of the size and composition of African populations before about two centuries ago. Surviving records from or about ancient African societies, with the exception of Egypt, are extremely rare. From the Middle Ages onward Arabs and, later, Europeans wrote accounts of their experiences in Africa. But the writings of these soldiers, traders, and explorers—while invaluable to historians—do not provide a full picture of the continent and are frequently colored by cultural biases.

THE FIRST BILLION ◆ ◆ ◆ AND BEYOND

Despite massive gaps in the archaeological and historical record—gaps that exist not only for Africa but to some extent for all regions of the world—the trajectory of African population growth can be inferred.

The earliest human societies consisted of small groups of hunter-gatherers. Their existence was precarious, with survival a constant struggle to find enough food in the face of such potentially life-threatening hazards as extreme weather conditions and attacks by wild animals. The unforgiving nature of this lifestyle took a harsh toll, severely limiting the size of human populations.

The development of agriculture, beginning in the Neolithic era some 10,000 years ago, marked a major turning point in human history. The domestication of plants and animals—which occurred independently in various regions of the world—produced a much larger and more reliable supply of food. It enabled people to live in settled communities and spurred an increase in human population. Still, the pace of world population growth was comparatively slow: it took until about A.D. 1804 for world population to reach 1 billion.

The San people of southern Africa, also known as Bushmen, continue to follow the hunter-gatherer lifestyle that characterized early human societies. The rigors of that lifestyle limited population growth.

Over the following two centuries, the rate of population growth accelerated dramatically. World population is estimated to have reached 2 billion in 1927, 3 billion in 1960, 4 billion in 1974, 5 billion in 1987, and 6 billion in 1999.

Population trends in Africa followed a similar pattern. Agriculture developed early on in the Nile Valley region of Egypt, which became the continent's major population center. Some scholars estimate that, by about 2,000 years ago, the Nile Valley contained approximately one-quarter of Africa's people. As the practice of farming and livestock raising gradually diffused from northern and western Africa southward, hunter-gatherer peoples adopted a more settled way of life and population expanded. But as elsewhere in the world, the rate of population growth in Africa was limited by various factors, including droughts, crop failures, disease, and warfare.

According to population estimates provided by the economic historian Angus Maddison in his book *The World Economy: A Millennial Perspective*, Africa's population grew from 16.5 million at the start of the first millennium to 33 million in the year 1000 and to 90.5 million in 1870. Thereafter, as was the case worldwide, the rate of population growth in Africa accelerated, with the most dramatic increases in the last half of the 20th century. By 2005 Africa's population stood at an estimated 906 million—a 10-fold increase since 1870 and 27 times higher than African population in the year 1000. Most significantly, Africa's population tripled over the last five decades of the 20th century.

This phenomenal change in the pace of population growth is not unique to Africa but reflects a global pattern. The last half of the 20th century saw world population explode. But the dividing line between the gradual population expansion that prevailed throughout most of human history and the rapid population growth of modern times can be drawn about the time of the Industrial Revolution. Beginning in England during the

18th century and then spreading to continental Europe and, eventually, the rest of the world, the Industrial Revolution was characterized by the application of steam-powered machinery to manufacturing processes. The implications for human society were profound. They included the movement of great numbers of people from rural to urban areas; a shift from subsistence farming and small-scale, family-based production to large-scale, factory-based production, which enabled the creation of surplus goods and the generation of unprecedented wealth; and an environment of accelerating innovation, which led to progress in numerous areas of human life. Taken together, the changes brought about by the Industrial Revolution helped lower mortality rates and increase birth rates, leading to significant growth in the world's population.

AFRICA AND THE WEST

During the period when it was transforming Western societies, the Industrial Revolution bypassed Africa. Among the most important reasons for this is the unequal relationship between Europe and Africa. Most infamously, that complex and controversial relationship included the transatlantic slave trade and, later, European colonization of Africa.

Between the early 16th century and the mid-19th century, an estimated 12 million to 26 million Africans were forcibly taken from the continent. Most were shipped west across the Atlantic Ocean, to work the farms and plantations of European colonies in North America, South America, and the Caribbean; perhaps 20 percent died during the grueling passage to the New World. In addition to these people, untold numbers died in the wars that were waged within Africa to generate captives for the slave trade.

Clearly, the slave trade had a significant impact on the population of Africa—though there is disagreement on the extent of that impact. Some historians and political scientists argue that

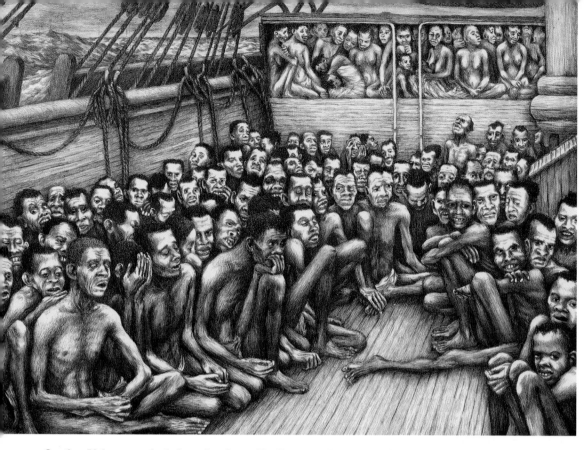

Captive Africans packed aboard a slave ship. Between the early 1500s and the mid-1800s, an estimated 12 million to 26 million Africans were forcibly taken from the continent to be sold as slaves in the New World.

the slave trade devastated Africa demographically in a way that went far beyond the huge numbers of people removed from the continent. That's because slaves were taken overwhelmingly from the ranks of the young and able-bodied. The loss of so many men and women in their childbearing years had an obvious effect on African population. But, some scholars argue, the slave trade also indirectly suppressed the number of people in the continent by stifling the development of African industry—and depriving the continent of the overall improvement in living conditions that would have resulted from industrialization. Many African historians bemoan the fact that while Europe's population more than doubled between the 17th and 19th centuries, providing essential labor for more industrial growth, Africa's population stagnated or even declined as a result of the slave trade. Yet other scholars insist that, while the loss of people through the slave trade significantly slowed down Africa's population growth, it probably did not cause a continent-wide stagnation or a decline in population. Angus Maddison, for example, believes that without the slave trade, Africa's population in the 18th century might have grown three times faster than it did.

The long-term population effects of European colonial encroachment into Africa—which took place mainly in the 19th century—are arguably even more difficult to quantify. European colonization did further undermine the capacity of African societies to achieve rapid economic growth by destroying local infant industries and exploiting the colonies as providers of raw materials needed by factories in European cities. And critics of colonialism often assert that one of the consequences of colonial rule was the neglect of indigenous food production, with dire outcome for the welfare of the African people. The late Guyanese historian Walter Rodney contended in his book *How Europe Underdeveloped Africa*, "Colonialism created conditions which led not just to periodic famine, but to chronic under-nourishment, malnutrition and deterioration in the physique of the African people."

Again, however, not all scholars believe that colonialism's effects were so straightforward. European colonialists did encourage local farmers to switch from subsistence farming to the cultivation of cash crops—such as coffee, cocoa, cotton, and palm oil—thereby undermining the capacity of Africans to feed themselves. But the production and export of cash crops became the main driver of economic growth in Africa during colonial rule, and even beyond. Growth in cash crop cultivation helped to expand and deepen Africa's agricultural sector. By boosting prosperity, albeit among a limited segment of the population, it probably also spurred population growth. Mortality rates tend to fall as people become relatively more prosperous and are able to

The question of how contact with the West affected African population levels is exceedingly complex. Obviously, the slave trade was a drain on population. But it was probably a slave ship that first brought the cassava (above, left) to Africa, and the plant—an excellent source of carbohydrates—grew well on the continent and sustained many African communities. Similarly, while European colonialists undermined Africa's ability to feed itself by encouraging the cultivation of cash crops such as cocoa, cotton, coffee, and oil palm (above, right), the export of those crops drove African economies for many years—and to the extent that increased general prosperity, it may also have increased population.

improve their food intake. The spread of modern medicine also contributed to the increase in population in Africa beginning in the colonial period.

POST-INDEPENDENCE POPULATION EXPLOSION

In the years after World War II (1939–1945), independence movements in Africa gained momentum. Within a decade of Ghana's independence from Britain in 1957, most of the continent had cast off colonial rule. This period saw a rapid rise in Africa's population—mirroring the dramatic post–World War II population increases in other parts of the developing world.

The industrialized nations, too, experienced a sharp increase in the number of babies born after the war—a phenomenon that came to be called the baby boom. However, its duration was limited (ending in the United States by 1964, for example) and its overall impact on population growth modest in comparison with population growth in the developing world. By the 1970s fertility rates in industrialized nations had slowed to levels close to or below the replacement rate of 2.1 children per woman. (Replacement-level fertility is the rate of children per woman necessary to keep the size of a particular population stable over a long period.) Population growth in Europe never exceeded 1 percent; in North America it rarely topped 1.5 percent. By the early years of the 21st century, the population growth rate for the industrialized world as a whole had dipped below 0.5 percent, with fertility rates of about 1.5 children per woman.

Gabonese dancers march in a celebration marking the anniversary of their country's independence (August 17). Like other African nations, Gabon has witnessed a very high rate of population growth since independence.

The experience of developing countries has been quite different. Overall population growth for these countries exceeded 2 percent a year during the late 1940s and 1950s, peaking at 2.4 percent during the 1960s. But for the least developed nations—most of which are in Africa—the population growth rate climbed above 2.5 percent during the mid-1990s before tailing off. Africa's population is currently growing at an annual rate of about 2 percent and is expected to average 1.7 percent during the period 2005–2050.

Africa's huge population growth in the six decades since World War II is attributable to two trends: declining mortality and, even more important, persistently high fertility. Mortality rates for Africans began falling noticeably during the closing years of colonial rule, and this trend picked up after independence. Between 1960 and 1982, crude death rate (the number of deaths per thousand persons) declined throughout Africa by an average of about 33 percent. In Kenya, for example, the crude death rate dropped by 50 percent, from 24 to 12. Other countries saw more modest gains; in Uganda the crude death rate fell by just 12 percent, from 21 to 19. At the same time, the number of babies who died before reaching their first birthday fell throughout the continent, and countries such as Botswana and South Africa saw infant mortality rates drop far below 100 deaths per 1,000 live births. The decline in death rates translated into higher life expectancy for Africans in the postwar years. In most countries on the continent, life expectancy rose well above 40 years, up from the low 30s in many cases.

Lower mortality rates and longer life spans were partly due to advances made in health care following increases in government social spending. Most of Africa's newly independent states allocated funds to build up their virtually nonexistent modern health systems. Thousands of health personnel were trained, with the result that in many African countries the ratio of doctors and

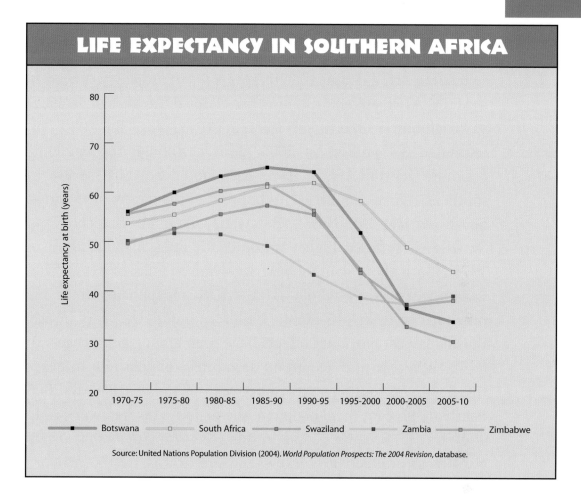

LIFE EXPECTANCY IN SOUTHERN AFRICA

Life expectancy at birth (years)

Botswana · South Africa · Swaziland · Zambia · Zimbabwe

Source: United Nations Population Division (2004). *World Population Prospects: The 2004 Revision,* database.

nurses to population rose significantly between 1960 and 1980. Though still inadequate by the standards of industrialized nations, improvements in health care facilities, especially in urban areas, enhanced the life chances of millions of Africans.

From the 1960s to the early 1980s, as death rates in Africa declined, birth rates also fell—but not by nearly as much. This led to rising population growth rates in most African countries, and in some places the acceleration was remarkable. For example, Sudan's annual population growth rate averaged 2.2 percent for the period 1960–1970 but 3.2 percent for the period 1970–1982; over the same years the average rate for Cameroon went from 2.0 percent to 3.0 percent, and for Kenya from 3.2 percent to 4.0 percent.

After the mid-1980s, mortality trends in much of Africa took a dramatic turn for the worse. Life expectancy stagnated—and in some areas even declined. This reversal can largely be traced to the HIV/AIDS epidemic, which has claimed the lives of as many as 20 million people in sub-Saharan Africa since the 1980s, an estimated 2.4 million in 2005 alone. Although the epidemic began in central Africa, its impact would be most severe in southern Africa. Countries in that part of the continent, such as South Africa, Zimbabwe, Botswana, Zambia, Lesotho, and Swaziland, suffered higher crude death rates in 2004 than in 1970. Throughout southern Africa—and to a lesser extent sub-Saharan Africa as a whole—HIV/AIDS is responsible for a significant rise in deaths among children under five years of age. But the largest mortality effects have been among adults aged 20 to 49. Whereas that age group accounted for just one in every five deaths in southern Africa between 1985 and 1990, in 2005 nearly 60 percent of all people in the region who died were 20 to 49 years old. Because people in this age group are among a society's most productive workers and are ordinarily the primary caregivers for children, the horrific effects of the HIV/AIDS epidemic have been greatly magnified, contributing to a host of economic and social problems.

In spite of the higher mortality rates produced by the HIV/AIDS epidemic, however, Africa's population continued to grow rapidly during the last decade of the 20th century and the first decade of the 21st. The most significant factor in this trend is continued high fertility rates in sub-Saharan Africa.

Overall, the average number of children born per woman in sub-Saharan Africa has declined over the past three and a half decades. According to World Bank statistics, total fertility for the region fell from 6.8 children per woman in 1970 to 4.9 children per woman in 2012. Still, 4.9 is more than twice the world fertility rate (2.4) and well above the rate of the regions with the next highest fertility (Latin America and the Caribbean, and North Africa and the Middle East, each with total fertility of 2.7).

In addition, the overall fertility rate for sub-Saharan Africa masks important differences among individual countries. World Bank statistics for 2013 show comparatively low to moderate fertility in countries such as Mauritius (1.78), South Africa (2.28), Namibia (2.41), Botswana (2.46), and Lesotho (2.89). On the other hand, fertility is extremely high in Niger (7.52), Uganda (6.65), Mali (6.35), Somalia (6.26), and Burundi (6.08). Generally, Africa's high-fertility countries tend to be among the continent's poorest nations, while the lower-fertility countries tend to be wealthier. This pattern is not unique to Africa; throughout the world, economic development and improvements in living standards have been followed by lower fertility rates.

POVERTY AND FERTILITY

There are a number of reasons why poor women have many children. First, in poor communities where everyday economic activities are labor intensive, families may decide to have more children to provide additional hands to share work. In poor rural areas children help their parents by performing a wide range of chores that have economic value, from gathering wood for burning to tending farm animals to simply looking after siblings, thereby freeing their mothers to work. In low-wage developing countries, children may have earning capacities that are close to, or even higher than, those of their mothers. In such cases, having more children is a way for families to increase their household incomes. In many African and Asian countries earnings by children constitute an important source of family income. Children engage in all sorts of commercial activities, from hawking goods on streets to working in sweatshops and toiling on plantations. Sometimes they engage in quite hazardous work such as mining. Sub-Saharan Africa has the

A street vendor at work, Libreville, Gabon. Earnings by children are an essential source of household income in many African countries. In fact, in some low-wage economies, children can make more money than their mothers—a powerful reason for African families to have many children.

highest incidence of child labor. According to the International Labour Organization's 2010 report *Accelerating Action Against Child Labour*, 28.4 percent of the region's child population is economically active—an increase since 2004.

A second reason why women in poor countries tend to have more babies is the increased likelihood that their offspring will die in childhood. Where infant and child mortality rates are high, especially in rural areas, parents may hope that if they have many children, at least some of those children will survive to adulthood. In sub-Saharan Africa, rates of infant and child mortality (death before age one and death before age five, respectively) have declined over the last decades. Yet they remain appallingly high. For every 1,000 infants born alive in sub-Saharan Africa, according to the World Health Organization, about 77 would not live to see their first birthday; for every 1,000 children under five years of age, 106 died. By comparison, in 2013 the countries of the European Union had an infant mortality rate of 8 per 1,000 live births and a child mortality rate of 13 per 1,000.

Third, in societies that lack social security, health insurance, or pension systems, the poor must often rely solely on their children to care for them in old age or in the event they become incapacitated by illness or accident. In most African societies, parents expect to depend on their children for support in their old age, and it is not uncommon for poor parents to expect to live with their children when they can no longer look after

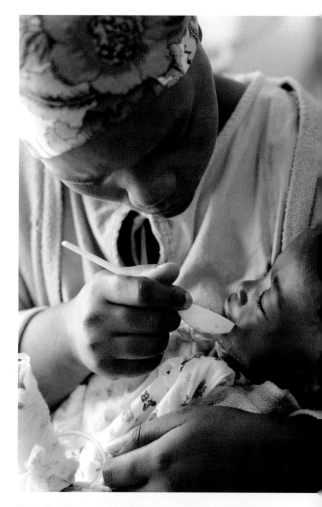

Africa's high rates of infant and child mortality contribute to high birth rates on the continent. Here a mother in Tugela Ferry, South Africa, attempts to feed her child, who is dying from AIDS.

themselves. This custom is by no means unique to Africa or to other developing regions; it was, in fact, widespread in Western countries before economic development enabled their citizens to live more independent lives or become reliant on the welfare state. In poor nations there are few trustworthy institutions such as banks, pensions, and insurance companies that help citizens to prepare for old age or possible infirmity by enabling them to save today for future consumption. Many African parents deem it safer to invest in their children for future benefits than to put their money into poorly managed local banks or other financial institutions, where the money may be subject to theft or may lose value because of inflation.

Fourth, traditional family structures—which remain intact in many African societies—tend to encourage large families. This is the case where early marriage is common, because early marriage means that girls start childbearing early in life. Using the results of a survey of young women aged 15–24, researchers estimated that about 42 percent of African girls are married before reaching the age of 18. As the United Nations Fund for Population Activities (UNFPA) reported, however, the rates of child marriage vary considerably by country. In Niger and the Democratic Republic of the Congo, for example, three-quarters of girls under 18 are married. According to the UNFPA, married adolescents face intense pressure to be pregnant. Adolescent fertility is increasingly viewed with concern by health care and family planning officials, as early childbearing is linked not only with higher rates of maternal and child mortality but also with conditions that serve to perpetuate high fertility and poverty, including loss of educational opportunities and lower future family income.

Fifth, lack of access to effective birth control—characteristic of many underdeveloped nations—is another reason for high fertility. Although use of modern contraceptives has risen in Africa

Family portrait, Conakry, Guinea. Traditional practices such as early marriage for girls and low contraceptive use contribute to high fertility in many African societies.

in recent decades, usage remains quite low. According to the 2005 UNFPA report, only 20 percent of married women in Africa use modern contraception, and just 27 percent use any kind of contraception. Rates in the United States, by comparison, are 71 percent and 76 percent, respectively. In developing nations the cost of purchasing modern contraceptives can put them out of the reach of the poorest in society, who are most likely to have large families. In Africa, on average, the poorest women are four times less likely to use contraception than the wealthiest. In some countries the proportion is 12 times lower. Cost is not the only reason for low contraceptive use, however. Lack of information about safe means of contraception may be a factor, and cultural or religious objections sometimes inhibit use of birth control devices as well.

LOOKING TO THE FUTURE

Over the first half of the 21st century, the UN Population Division projects a steady decline in total fertility for Africa. On the basis of a medium scenario, for example, the Population Division's report *World Population Prospects: The 2010 Revision* found Africa's fertility rate to be 4.64 in 2005–2010, and projected that the rate would fall to 3.59 in 2025–2030 and 2.89 in 2045–2050. A similar decline is projected for the sub-Saharan region, although fertility there is expected to remain slightly higher than in the continent as a whole (3.00 in 2045–2050).

By mid-century, Africa's fertility rates will have moved closer to the projected rates for the world as a whole (2.17); for other developing regions, such as Asia (1.88) and Latin America and the Caribbean (1.79); and for developed regions such as Europe (1.91). Still, Africa's population is projected to grow by an average of 1.69 percent annually between 2005 and 2050, outstripping rates for all other regions of the world, and doubling the number of people on the continent.

It is perhaps difficult to understand why Africa's population can be projected to double during the first 50 years of the 21st century even as its total fertility rate is expected to fall by nearly 50 percent during the same period. The apparent anomaly is explained largely by the age characteristics of Africa's population. Africa has a younger population than any other region of the world. In 2013, according to the UN Population Division, an estimated 41.5 percent of all Africans were under 15 years of age (compared with 28.2 percent for the world as a whole, and just 15.9 percent for Europe). In succeeding years, this cohort of young people will enter their childbearing years, ensuring a huge number of new births and fueling the steep rise in Africa's population.

Within Africa, population growth over the next decades is expected to be uneven. Some of the poorest countries on the continent will experience the most rapid growth, with the size of their populations nearly quadrupling between 2000 and 2050. They include the Democratic Republic of the Congo, Ethiopia, Uganda, Angola, and Niger. By contrast, countries experiencing little population growth will include some of Africa's wealthier nations, including South Africa and Mauritius. Botswana and Lesotho are both expected to have fewer people by 2050, in part because of the toll taken by HIV/AIDS.

3 RURAL AFRICA

Since the middle of the 20th century, when 7 of every 10 people on earth lived in rural areas, the world's population has steadily become more urban. The year 2007 marked the first time in human history that more people worldwide lived in cities and densely populated towns than in rural areas.

While Africa, too, is experiencing a population shift toward urban areas, it remains the most rural of continents. In 2013, according to the United Nations Population Division, an estimated 62 percent of Africa's people lived in rural areas. But the proportion varied significantly by region. Northern Africa, for example, had a little less than half (48.9 percent) of its population in rural areas in 2013. In sub-Saharan Africa, the rate was 64.8 percent overall, with a significantly higher percentage in Eastern Africa (77.9 percent) than in Western Africa (57.6 percent) or Southern Africa (43.7 percent).

It must be noted that, for demographic purposes, there are no precise, universally accepted definitions of the terms *rural* and *urban*. As the UN acknowledges, "Because of national differences in the characteristics which distinguish urban from rural areas, the distinction between urban and rural population is not amenable to a single definition applicable to all countries." Rural areas, however, are usually less densely populated than urban areas and—particularly in developing countries—generally continue to be characterized by the agriculturally based lifestyle of a significant proportion of their inhabitants. Urban areas, by contrast, generally have larger concentrations of people than do rural areas and, in developing countries, tend to provide a higher standard of living for inhabitants.

In 2013 rural dwellers comprised about 6 in 10 of all people in Asia, making it the only continent other than Africa where less than half the population lives in cities and large towns. Rural populations are decidedly smaller in the world's more developed regions, such as Western Europe (23.0 percent) and Northern America, which comprises mainly the United States and Canada (19.3 percent).

RURAL POVERTY

For Americans the countryside may conjure up idyllic images of fertile land, bountiful harvests, and a healthy and wholesome way of life. In much of Africa, the reality of rural life is quite different. Continent-wide, more than 7 in 10 of Africa's poor people live in rural areas; many continually face a grim struggle to eke out an existence from land that is of declining fertility, prone to droughts, and subject to infestation by destructive pests. The basic infrastructure considered necessary for a decent standard

A farmer plows his parched fields near Tobruk, Libya. In Northern Africa, about half the population lives in rural areas, compared with more than three-quarters in Eastern Africa and nearly two-thirds in the sub-Saharan part of the continent as a whole. Almost everywhere on the continent, though, rural dwellers suffer high rates of poverty as they try to earn a living from land whose fertility may be on the decline.

of living is woefully lacking. For example, only a small minority of Africa's rural villagers—2 percent, according to one recent estimate—are connected to national power grids. Less than half of Africans in rural areas have access to sanitation or to safe water, making them highly vulnerable to debilitating and often deadly waterborne diseases such as cholera, dysentery, and typhoid fever.

The persistence of grinding poverty in rural Africa is in part a result of the decades-long decline of rural economies, and especially of the poor performance of agricultural sectors in many African countries. In sub-Saharan Africa, the majority of the labor force is engaged in agriculture (though this is not true of all countries in the region), mostly in small-scale and subsistence farming. Thus, agricultural failures tend to have especially severe consequences—including food shortages and widespread hunger. Among the sub-Saharan African countries that have faced food emergencies in recent years are Burundi, Chad, Ethiopia, Kenya, Malawi, Mozambique, Niger, Zambia, and Zimbabwe.

Overall, agricultural food production in sub-Saharan Africa has grown since the mid-1970s, but not by enough to keep pace with the region's expanding population. (Again, however, this is not the case with all countries in sub-Saharan Africa, some of which have managed to maintain adequate levels of agricultural production.) During the period 1975–1985, food output per capita in sub-Saharan Africa declined by 1.6 percent; it fell by 0.4 percent in 1985–1994 and was even during the period 1995–2002. Sub-Saharan Africa is the only developing-country region where agricultural production has failed to keep up with population growth for most of the last three decades.

With Africa's small-scale and subsistence farmers, a low level of technology is the rule. Seen here: rice farmers in Uganda.

The reasons for sub-Saharan Africa's agricultural difficulties are multiple, and they vary by country.

Kenyan villagers await the distribution of food aid. Kenya's worst drought in recorded history had a devastating effect on farmers and pastoralists, but many observers also blame government neglect of rural development for exacerbating the natural disaster.

To begin, much of the region's land is not naturally well suited for intensive farming or livestock raising. This is the case, for example, in Africa's tropical areas, where soil is less fertile than is soil in temperate zones. It is also the case with the Sahel—the semiarid belt that runs across Africa south of the Sahara and north of the savanna and wooded grassland of central Africa, extending from Senegal in the west through Mauritania, Mali, Burkina Faso, Niger, northern Nigeria, Chad, Sudan, Ethiopia, Kenya, and Somalia. The Sahel is subject to severe droughts, which have plunged affected nations into food crises. In Sahel countries like Niger and Mali, such crises have been compounded by fertility rates that rank among the highest on the planet. Agricultural experts believe that, even with the efficient use of available technology, these nations would lack the capacity to feed their populations.

The situation in Kenya, where the country's worst drought in history brought millions to the brink of starvation, is somewhat different. More than 80 percent of Kenya's land is arid and semiarid, and almost one-third of the country's people live on this land, relying for their survival largely on their herds of livestock or on small-scale farming. While it is not surprising that the absence of normal seasonal rains in five of the six years between 1999 and 2005 imperiled the livelihood of these people, development experts argue that the difficulties were greatly exacerbated by long-standing Kenyan government policies toward rural areas. According to the charity organization Oxfam, years of economic and political marginalization have resulted in the arid and semiarid lands being the most underdeveloped areas of Kenya. These areas have the highest percentage of people living below the poverty line and the lowest access to basic services in the country. This chronic neglect, explains Oxfam, has eroded the ability of local communities to cope with recurrent droughts, resulting in declining agricultural output and increasing poverty.

More government investment and better land management, development experts believe, could enable Kenya's small-scale farmers and pastoralists to maintain a decent livelihood—and make substantially larger contributions to the national economy.

In other areas of Africa, the needs of a growing population have contributed to a decline in the capacity of the land to provide sustenance. Unsustainable farming has depleted soil fertility, resulting in falling crop yields. Overgrazing of livestock and excessive cutting of trees (often for firewood) have stripped land of vegetation, leading to erosion and desertification. About half of the farmland in sub-Saharan Africa suffers to some extent from

In many parts of Africa, deforestation has led to soil erosion and desertification. In this photo from Madagascar, a patch of wooded land is being burned to make room for more farmland.

soil erosion, and as much as 80 percent of crop and grazing land shows some form of degradation. According to the United Nations, about 1.2 billion acres (500 million hectares) of African land suffers moderate to severe degradation.

Unfortunately, population pressures and overuse of land form only part of the problem. Changes in climatic conditions have expanded the areas affected by land degradation, and have increased the severity of that degradation. One of the areas most dramatically affected by climate change is the Sahara Desert, where already hot temperatures are rising and available water supplies diminishing. Perhaps more worrying, the desert has been advancing southward at an alarming rate, forcing more and more people to abandon their homes and migrate in search of fertile land. Desertification has contributed to poor crop yields

This canal, which was supposed to carry water from Lake Chad to irrigate farms in northeastern Nigeria, is emblematic of the dismal state of rural infrastructure in Africa.

and food shortages in Africa's most populous nation. In 2000 Sanni Zango Daura, then Nigeria's environment minister, said food production in northern Nigeria was being hampered by the southward expansion of the desert at a rate of 0.37 miles (0.6 kilometers) per year.

Climatic conditions in Africa are expected to deteriorate in coming years, placing increasing pressure on the region's growing population. A 2008 report by the United Nations Food and Agriculture Organization said that the most severe impact of climate change was likely to be felt in sub-Saharan African countries least able to handle the effects of the worsening conditions. The report found that Africa and South Asia are the regions most vulnerable to climate change. It is projected that Africa's average annual rainfall will decrease, and that the area of land with a growing period of less than 120 days will expand over the next 50 years. By 2080, the report projects, some 75 percent of Africa's population could be at risk of hunger. This may force a redistribution of some of Africa's vulnerable populations.

MISMANAGEMENT AND INSTABILITY

While difficult natural conditions have contributed to Africa's food and agricultural production problems, these have been compounded by poor management of available land and water resources as well as political instability. Agriculture accounts for just under two-thirds of employment in sub-Saharan Africa (with women making up nearly half the workforce in the sector), yet it has failed to receive a level of government and private sector investment commensurate with its importance to African economies and the well-being of African peoples.

Since independence, Africa's ruling classes have focused their attention on building urban centers as the foundations of modernity. Worse, this modernization has often been financed largely with resources extracted from the rural areas. Political rulers and the urban elites used various methods to squeeze the rural population, including the underpricing of locally grown food and the imposition of direct and indirect taxes on agricultural production.

Rural communities have also suffered as a result of political instability in African countries, often triggered by struggles for national resources between competing factions of the elites. Many of Africa's civil wars have been fought in rural areas, where rebel groups have tended to set up base. The brutality of combatants, who often rape and pillage their way through rural communities, has forced millions of people to flee their villages to seek safety in cities and towns. People left behind in war-affected areas face risks in attending to their land. Understandably, their precarious condition may make them reluctant to invest in the development of their agricultural land.

Only a few African nations have large commercial farming sectors, operated as modern businesses with the goal of maximizing market share and profit. In some areas plantations cultivate export crops such as palm oil, rubber, tea, and cocoa, which are often linked to processing operations of multinational corporations. But the vast majority of African farmers are small-scale subsistence growers, who seek first to produce enough food to feed their family and then grow cash crops to earn money to pay for other provisions.

Most subsistence farmers in Africa still rely on basic tools. They also use much less fertilizer per acre than growers in other developing regions. Similarly, the use of modern chemicals such as pesticides and herbicides to control pests, diseases, and weeds is minimal. Most farmers depend on rain to feed their crops, as barely 6 percent of total cultivated land is under irrigation (compared, for example, with one-third of cultivated in Asia).

The low level of technology of African farming partly reflects the fact that most farmers are too poor to invest in more advanced technology to achieve greater efficiency. But this situation is also tied to the structure of the farming sector. The land tenure systems in many African countries do not encourage or facilitate investment in agriculture. In many parts of the continent, land is under state or communal ownership and there are weak property rights. Because land is often divided between members of the family or clan, there has also been considerable fragmentation of land, with individual plots becoming smaller and smaller over time.

Without sizeable holdings and secure property rights, farmers lack the incentive to invest in developing their production capabilities and capacities. Many African governments and regional economic institutions recognize the importance of improving land management, in particular the need to improve access to land and security of land rights to encourage private investment in agriculture and rural development. But implementing land reform can be tricky in places where there is strong belief in communalism and private land ownership is an emotive issue, underlying much social conflict.

Poor rural infrastructure also hampers agricultural development in Africa. Farms located far

Workers collect apples at a large fruit-growing concern in South Africa's Western Cape Province. South Africa is one of the few nations on the continent that has a large commercial agriculture sector.

HIV/AIDS AND THE RURAL LABOR SHORTAGE

HIV/AIDS has exacted a horrific human toll in both rural and urban areas of sub-Saharan Africa. But its economic impact is arguably more evident in rural areas, where medical facilities are most lacking.

UNAIDS, the Joint United Nations Programme on HIV/AIDS, says AIDS has killed more than 28 million people worldwide since the first cases were reported in 1981. Two-thirds of the 60 countries in the world highly affected by HIV/AIDS are in sub-Saharan Africa, with the largest concentration in southern Africa. In 2012 sub-Saharan Africa accounted for 23.5 million out of 33.8 million people in the world estimated to be living with HIV, the retrovirus that leads to AIDS. The number of deaths from AIDS in sub-Saharan Africa in 2012 was estimated at 1.2 million, out of a global total of 1.7 million. The epidemic is largely responsible for making Africa the only major region in the world to have experienced a decline in life expectancy since the late 1980s. The extent of the drop in life expectancy in the most HIV/AIDS-affected countries is mind-boggling. For example, in Botswana, where HIV prevalence was estimated at 36 percent of the adult population in 2012, life expectancy has fallen from 65 years in 1985 to 53 years in 2012. In southern Africa as a whole, life expectancy has fallen from 61 years to 51 years over the same period.

In Africa, where HIV transmission is largely through heterosexual contact, women are infected with the virus at younger ages and in greater numbers than

from road networks face enormous difficulties and high costs getting their produce to market. It is estimated that almost two-thirds of African farmers are effectively cut off from national and international markets because of inadequate transport infrastructure. Poor storage facilities and lack of processing capacity can also lead to large post-harvest losses.

AGING OF THE RURAL POPULATION

The many difficulties associated with agriculture in sub-Saharan Africa have contributed to an exodus, predominantly of young men. This gender dimension of the epidemic is important for agricultural development, since women play such a crucial role in small-scale farming in Africa.

Perhaps more significant for agriculture and other economic production in Africa, however, is the age distribution of HIV/AIDS victims. The disease hits most people in the prime of their working lives. For example, whereas during 1985–1990 period, deaths in southern Africa of adults aged 20 to 49 accounted for only 20 percent of all deaths, by 2012 nearly 60 percent of all deaths occurred within this age group. This dramatic change in the age distribution of mortality is expected to have a major impact on the age distribution of populations of AIDS-affected countries.

Apart from depressing population growth, HIV/AIDS undermines the productivity of those living with the disease. The debilitating effects of the disease mean that an increasing segment of the labor force is too infirm to work or perform their tasks effectively. It is estimated that farm output can fall by as much as 50 percent in HIV/AIDS-affected households, largely because of a shortage of labor to work agricultural plots. The FAO has estimated that in the 25 worst-affected African countries, AIDS has killed 7 million agricultural workers since 1985 and could kill 12 million more by 2020. The organization also says that the size of sub-Saharan Africa's agricultural labor force could fall by up to 25 percent by 2020 as a result of the epidemic.

people, from rural areas. This has pushed up the median age of the rural population.

It has also contributed to a shortage of agricultural labor in many countries, despite high population growth. In certain areas, the scarcity of able-bodied farm workers is greatly exacerbated by the HIV/AIDS epidemic. But even in some rural districts that have not been hard-hit by HIV/AIDS or seen a large exodus of young people, farmers complain of an agricultural labor shortage. Largely because farm wages tend to be low, young people who remain in rural areas are increasingly seeking means of livelihood other than manual labor on farms.

URBANIZATION

I f Africa is the continent with the most rural of populations, it also is the continent undergoing the fastest rate of urbanization—and that trend is expected to continue. Spurred largely by the influx of young people from rural regions, Africa's urban areas are growing at a sometimes dizzying pace.

In 2000–2010 Africa's urban population grew at an average annual rate of about 3.6 percent, compared with 2.7 percent for Asia. Many cities in the continent have grown at an annual rate of 5 to 6 percent, and some by as much as 10 percent. By 2013 over 400 million Africans—more than 40 percent of the continent's population—lived in urban areas. In nine countries of sub-Saharan Africa, a majority of the population lived in cities or urban areas.

INDUSTRIALIZATION AND URBANIZATION

One of the most striking developments in the world during the past 200 years has been the

(Opposite) A crowded street, Kampala. The Ugandan capital tripled in size between 1975 and 2003. Such explosive growth has been seen in many other African cities, particularly national capitals, over the last few decades.

mass movement of people from rural to urban areas. This was arguably one of the main consequences of the Industrial Revolution, which transformed agriculturally based societies into factory-driven, industrially based societies.

The concentration of people in cities and large towns resulted from two sets of considerations, known as pull and push factors. Pull factors are the attractions of urban life, such as better job prospects and access to greater educational or cultural opportunities. Push factors are the negative aspects of rural life, such as the difficulties of making a living by farming and underdeveloped infrastructure. The advancements in science and technology that were the hallmark of the Industrial Revolution, especially in the use of energy, created pull and push factors for urbanization. Factory centers required large pools of skilled and unskilled labor, attracting workers with the prospect of increased earnings and greater prosperity. At the same time, the application of technology in agriculture enabled the same amount of farming output to be achieved with much less manual labor, pushing farm workers away from rural areas and toward the cities.

THE GROWTH OF AFRICA'S CITIES

The process of industrialization was later in coming to Africa, and Africa has not yet felt the effects of technological change to the extent that these effects have been felt in Europe or the Americas. Nevertheless, beginning in the late 19th century—and particularly since the mid-1900s—technological advancements, economic changes, and infrastructure development have pulled and pushed more Africans toward urban areas.

The proportion of the continent's population living in urban areas has risen steadily over the last half century. In 1950 an estimated 14.7 percent of Africa's people lived in urban areas, according to the UN Population Division. By 1970 the figure stood at 23.4 percent; by 1990 it had climbed to 32 percent. In 2012 urban dwellers made up an estimated 40 percent of Africa's people, slightly less than the proportion in Asia (39.8 percent). Africa's urban population is projected to rise to 53.5 percent by 2030 (and Asia's to 54.5 percent). This would make Africa about as urbanized as Europe was in 1955. By 2030, meanwhile, Europe's urban population is projected to reach 78.3 percent, and Northern America's to 86.7 percent.

In most African countries, urbanization has involved the concentration of large segments of the population in the capital city. A handful of national capitals in Africa now hold between 20 percent and 30 percent of their country's entire population. These include Brazzaville, Republic of the Congo; Accra, Ghana; and Tunis, Tunisia. Tripoli, the capital of Libya, is home to more than one in three people in the North African country.

Nigeria and South Africa are unusual among African countries. In 2003, according to the United Nations Population Division, South Africa had four and Nigeria five urban agglomerations with 1 million or more people. (An urban agglomeration consists of a city or, in some cases, more than one city, along with suburbs and highly settled adjacent areas.) Most other African nations had no more than two major cities.

Before the end of colonial rule, however, there were few major

Lagos, a sprawling urban agglomeration whose population exceeded 12 million in 2013, is the world's fastest-growing megacity. Rapid, unplanned growth in Nigeria's financial and commercial capital has led to a host of problems, including woefully inadequate sanitation facilities.

AFRICAN URBAN AGGLOMERATIONS OF 1 MILLION OR MORE, 2013

Agglomeration	Population	Agglomeration	Population
Cairo, Egypt	11.00 million	Mbuji-Mayi, DRC	1.49 million
Lagos, Nigeria	10.60 million	Lusaka, Zambia	1.45 million
Kinshasa, DRC	8.75 million	Pretoria, SA	1.43 million
Mogadishu, Somalia	6.40 million	Hargeisa, Somalia	1.34 million
Khartoum, Sudan	5.20 million	Brazzaville, Congo	1.32 million
Luanda, Angola	4.80 million	Benin, Nigeria	1.30 million
Alexandria, Egypt	4.40 million	Vereeniging, SA	1.14 million
Abidjan, Ivory Coast	4.13 million	Tunis, Tunisia	1.11 million
Johannesburg, SA	3.67 million	Maiduguri, Nig.	1.10 million
Nairobi, Kenya	3.50 million	Pt Harcourt, Nig.	1.10 million
Cape Town, SA	3.40 million	Fès, Morocco	1.10 million
Kano, Nigeria	3.40 million	Zaria, Nigeria	1.03 million
Dar es Salaam, Tanz.	3.35 million	Huambo, Angola	1.03 million
Casablanca, Morocco	3.28 million	Ogbomosho, Nig.	1.03 million
Addis Ababa, Ethiopia	2.93 million	Freetown, SL	1.00 million
Durban, SA	2.88 million		
Dakar, Senegal	2.86 million		
Ibadan, Nigeria	2.84 million		
Algiers, Algeria	2.80 million		
Accra, Ghana	2.34 million		
Tripoli, Libya	2.26 million		
Douala, Cameroon	2.13 million		
Abuja, Nigeria	2.00 million		
Ouagadougou, B. Faso	1.90 million		
Antananarivo, Mad.	1.90 million		
Kumasi, Ghana	1.83 million		
Rabat, Morocco	1.80 million		
Yaoundé, Cameroon	1.80 million		
Bamako, Mali	1.70 million		
Maputo, Mozambique	1.66 million		
Conakry, Guinea	1.65 million		
Harare, Zimbabwe	1.63 million		
Kampala, Uganda	1.60 million		
Kaduna, Nigeria	1.56 million		
Lubumbashi, DRC	1.54 million		

Source: United Nations Population Division, 2013.

cities anywhere in Africa. The largest urban agglomerations on the continent in 1960 were the Egyptian cities of Cairo (with 3.8 million residents) and Alexandria (1.5 million), as well as Johannesburg, South Africa (1.5 million). Today 50 African cities have populations of 1 million or more, and two—Cairo and Lagos, Nigeria—qualify as megacities (agglomerations with 10 million or more). In 1960, at the time of independence, the Nigerian capital had only 762,000 inhabitants. By 2012 Lagos was a sprawling urban agglomeration of some 10.6 million. The city continues to grow rapidly, and by 2025 it is expected to be the world's ninth most populous urban agglomeration, with 17 million people.

A pall of smog enshrouds Cairo. The Egyptian capital is one of the world's most congested and polluted cities.

As is true elsewhere in the world, the rapid growth of African cities has frequently been accompanied by a host of problems. The influx of new residents strains—and often overwhelms—existing infrastructure and government services. This is especially the case because infrastructure and services such as electricity, water and sanitation, housing, police protection, and educational institutions are already stretched thin in many African nations.

THE EXPLOSION OF SLUMS

A highly visible sign of Africa's rapid urbanization is the development and expansion of slums—areas of residence characterized by poverty, overcrowding, and inadequate and substandard facilities such as durable housing, clean water, and sanitation.

According to the United Nations Human Settlements Programme, known as UN-HABITAT, the world's slums are growing and will increasingly become the centers of poverty in developing countries. "The locus of global poverty is moving to cities, a process now recognised as the urbanisation of poverty," observed United Nations Secretary-General Kofi Annan in the foreword to UN-HABITAT's 2003 global report, *The Challenge of Slums.*

In its latest report, *State of the World's Cities 2012-13*, UN-HABITAT says slum dwellers account for 41 percent of the population of developing regions, compared with just 6 percent in developed regions. Sub-Saharan Africa has the highest concentration of slum dwellers: in 2013, according to the UN-HABITAT report, 62 percent of the people in the region's urban areas were living in slums. This was far higher than the second-highest region, South Asia, where 35 percent live in slums. Sub-Saharan Africa also has the world's highest annual slum growth rate, which at 4.53 percent is just below the region's annual rate of urban growth (4.58 percent). UN-HABITAT warns that the

In sub-Saharan Africa, according to UN-HABITAT, nearly three-quarters of all urban residents live in a slum. Here, a mother carries her child across a drainage canal in a slum area of Nairobi, Kenya.

problems posed by slums are likely to worsen as the world's rural population has peaked and as further population growth will be absorbed mostly by urban settlements.

In the West, slums are usually neighborhoods that were initially of adequate standards but became dilapidated and overcrowded following the exodus of wealthier inhabitants and the influx of poorer ones. However, in Africa and Asia slums are mainly places that lack resources from the beginning. In some cases Third World slums develop around poorly planned government housing estates, but more often they start as collections of shacks erected by poor people on the outskirts of urban areas. The inhabitants of these makeshift settlements—who in many cases are squatters— typically have little or no access to running water, sanitation, or electricity.

Everywhere in the world, slums are overcrowded and neglected areas marked by intense poverty and inferior and often appalling living conditions. They are places associated with high levels of disease, crime, drug abuse, and prostitution. In cities where decent housing is in short supply and expensive, most low-paid workers and the unemployed have few alternatives to living in slum districts. As such, these impoverished areas are home to a wide range of inhabitants, from low-paid state employees to domestic workers and the jobless.

The absence of decent housing conditions is probably what most characterizes slums anywhere in the world. According to UN-HABITAT, over 100 million people in Africa live in overcrowded conditions, defined as four or more persons sharing a small room. Only South Asia has more people living in such appalling conditions. Poor housing invariably comes with inadequate public services. For example, only 80 percent of sub-Saharan Africa's urban population had access to safe water, and just below 40 percent got water from a tap. Bad water means that people are much more susceptible to water-borne diseases. According to UN-HABITAT, people in sub-Saharan Africa spend at least one-third of their incomes on treating water-related diseases such as cholera, dysentery, and other diarrheal illnesses.

All in all, life for slum dwellers anywhere in the world is much tougher than for other city residents. Slum residents are more likely to live shorter lives, suffer more hunger and disease, obtain less education, and have fewer job opportunities than non-slum urban residents.

THE ATTRACTION OF CITIES

When considering the plight of the urban poor in Africa, several crucial facts must be borne in mind. Although they are certainly deprived by developed-nation standards—and they are deprived in comparison to urban middle classes and elites in their own countries—many of Africa's urban poor have access to higher levels of public services than do the continent's rural poor. Cities are growing in size and becoming increasingly overcrowded largely because life in impoverished rural villages is even more difficult than life in impoverished inner cities.

Most indicators of poverty show that people who live in rural areas are more likely to lack basic public services than are urban dwellers. For instance, according to the World Bank's 2012 World Development Indicators report, 79 percent of the urban population in sub-Saharan Africa had access to improved sanitation facilities in 2012, an increase from 55 percent just six years earlier. And this regional average masks even greater disparities in certain countries. In Niger, for example, 34 percent of urban dwellers had access to improved sanitation, but only 4 percent of rural residents had such access. In Liberia the rates were 29 percent in urban areas and 7 percent in rural areas; in Angola, 85 percent in cities and towns and 16 percent in the countryside.

Similar disparities exist for access to improved water. In 2012 more than 400 million Africans in rural areas lacked access to improved water, but less than 75 million were lacking in urban areas.

African cities face severe shortages of other infrastructure services, such as electricity and roads, but many rural areas are simply not connected to any existing networks. While poor

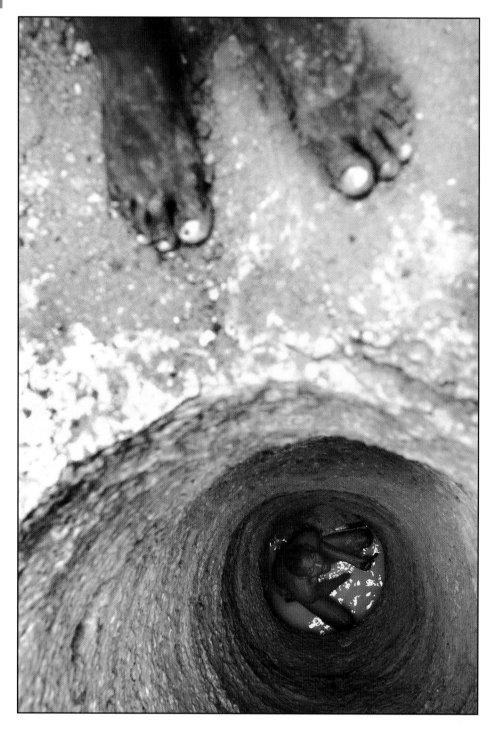

Life in urban slums may be filled with difficulties and deprivations, but poor Africans continue to gravitate to cities in large part because conditions in rural areas are even worse. Here a rural villager in northeastern Kenya must dig deep for water after drought has dried up wells in the area.

slum dwellers in large cities can tap electricity supplies, legally or illegally, this is not possible in rural areas remote from the national grid. Sub-Saharan Africa has the worst rural access to roads among developing regions, with many communities located miles from the nearest road.

Perhaps most important, cities have jobs—or at least provide an environment in which people can eke out a living for themselves. The majority of the employment opportunities in Africa's cities are poorly paid and do not come with employment protection or insurance coverage, but this state of affairs is preferable for many young people who have rejected work on the land.

The majority of people in African cities and towns work in the informal sector, also known as the informal economy. This comprises economic activities that are unregulated and unrecorded by government. Sub-Saharan Africa is the region with the highest proportion of its labor force working in the informal sector. According to the International Labour Organisation (ILO), informal employment makes up 72 percent of non-agricultural employment in sub-Saharan Africa (compared with 65 percent in Asia).

Types of activities conducted in the informal economy vary enormously, ranging from small-scale manufacturing to services such as hairdressing, car repair, and money changing. Basically, any business that can be conducted on a small scale without attracting the attention of the authorities can be found in the informal sector of African economies. The United Nations Economic Commission for Africa estimates that about two-thirds of African families are sustained by the informal sector, either as operators or indirectly as beneficiaries of its services.

5 MIGRATION

Each year, millions of people migrate from their homelands to other countries. Migrants may be motivated by various factors, but among the most important is economic opportunity. It is therefore not surprising that worldwide, the flow of migrants is primarily in the direction of developed countries from poorer areas.

The number of people leaving Africa consistently surpasses the number migrating into the continent from other regions. Between 2000 and 2005, according to the UN Population Division, an average of 455,000 more people left Africa annually than arrived from other areas. That number declined somewhat, to 366,000 annually for the period 2005–2010. By mid-century the number is projected to be 322,000.

BRAIN DRAIN:

For a continent with nearly a billion people and a high fertility rate, a net annual loss of several hundred thousand people to migration can hard-

(Opposite) Seeking safety, political freedom, or better economic opportunities in the developed world, hundreds of thousands of people emigrate from Africa every year. This would-be migrant is living in a forest in Morocco, awaiting an opportunity to cross into the Spanish enclave of Melilla—a gateway for many Africans hoping for a better life in Europe.

ly be considered a major factor in population trends. And in fact, as a percentage of Africa's total population, the level of migration out of the continent is actually less today than it was in the 1950s. What makes migration a concern for many African governments and international development institutions, however, is the kind of people who are now leaving. Because rich nations now generally restrict in-migration of unskilled and semi-skilled workers, a higher percentage of skilled people are probably leaving Africa today than previously did.

In the view of many African leaders and development specialists, the migration to developed nations of large numbers of highly trained African professionals such as doctors, engineers, and academics—a process referred to as "brain drain"—is robbing African nations of the knowledge, skills, and entrepreneurial leadership they require to emerge from underdevelopment. In its *2005 Economic Report on Africa*, the UN Economic Commission for Africa (ECA) cited data showing that the emigration of highly skilled people from Africa rose from an average of 1,800 per year during the period 1960–1975 to 23,000 per year during the period 1984–1987. More than half of the Africans who went abroad to study physics and chemistry in the 1960s, for example, stayed overseas, according to the report.

This brain drain, the ECA asserts, has retarded economic progress and hurt living standards in a variety of ways. First, by reducing the supply of skilled and professional labor, the brain drain has undermined the growth of unskilled and semi-skilled jobs in abandoned countries. This is because it exacerbates the shortage of managerial staff needed for firms to operate and provide employment to general workers. For instance, it is estimated that 50,000 to 60,000 middle- and high-level managers emigrated from Africa in the period 1986–1990. In the absence of qualified replacements, the loss of these managers would also mean the loss of the jobs they would have supervised had they stayed

A doctor in Sierra Leone examines his patient. Like other African countries, Sierra Leone has seen many of its trained medical professionals emigrate. A 2002 report, for example, indicated that there were more Sierra Leonean doctors in the Chicago area than in all of Sierra Leone.

home. The exodus of talented people is also said to deny poor countries some of their potentially most enterprising and ambitious people, thereby forestalling the rise of a strong entrepreneurial class that could spearhead full-scale industrialization.

But the biggest complaint made by anti-poverty groups is that the brain drain undermines essential public services in poor countries, such as health care. It is said that while people in Africa die of curable ailments because of shortages in medical staff, thousands of Africa-trained doctors and nurses work abroad, mainly in rich countries. Anti-poverty campaigners claim that the extent of the drain of Africa's scarce human resources to the West is an indictment of the global economic system. It is pointed out, for instance, that there are more Ethiopian and Nigerian doctors working in the United States than in their homelands. In Ghana and Zimbabwe three-quarters of all doctors are said to emigrate within a few years of finishing their medical training.

African governments complain that the brain drain is increasingly costing their countries large sums of money invested in the training of professionals. Furthermore, they say, it is undermining their efforts to achieve the Millennium Development Goals, or MDGs—eight key development-related objectives that were adopted by UN member states in 2000 and are supposed to be attained by 2015—such as ending extreme poverty, achieving universal primary education, reducing child mortality, and improving maternal health. South Africa, for instance, claims to have spent $1 billion educating health workers who migrated, a sum equivalent to about one-third of all development aid the country received between 1994 and 2000. Some people regard such non-yielding investment as tantamount to poor countries subsidizing rich nations.

◆ ◆ ◆ OR BRAIN GAIN?

Yet the impact of the migration of educated and talented people from poor to rich nations may not be so clear-cut. While some economists share the view that this migration is detrimental, others argue that the effects are more complicated

In this class for immigrants to Spain, a young African learns how to tell time.

than the term *brain drain* suggests. Temporary migration of people to more economically advanced countries may, in the long run, enhance the technological capabilities of the sending country because while they are abroad, migrants pick up knowledge and develop skills that can be useful on their return home. Migration is one means of international technological transfer. For example, the remarkable pace of economic growth in China in recent decades is partly due to the crucial contribution of Chinese expatriates, who returned home not only with financial resources but also with new ideas and connections in overseas markets.

Migrants also contribute to their homeland through the remittances they send to relatives and other associates back home. In 2012, according to the World Bank, sub-Saharan Africa received from overseas workers more than $20 billion in formally transferred remittances—more than ten times the amount received in 1990. Nigeria was the largest beneficiary, receiving perhaps one-third of the total. But the true value of remittances to sub-Saharan Africa is considerably higher than $20 billion, as not all nations track and report remittances, and many migrants also use informal channels to send money back home. Accounting for untraceable nonformal remittances, sub-Saharan Africa may have received $30 billion or more from migrants in 2012.

Furthermore, one of the main reasons developing countries lose so many of their highly qualified people is the lack of opportunities at home. The brain drain is largely a symptom of problems within the sending countries, such as low pay for professionals, shortages of facilities for specialists, corruption, and political instability. If migration were arbitrarily stopped—by either the sending or receiving countries—this would not necessarily resolve the staffing shortages of public services in Africa, since their problems stem mainly from inadequate funds to employ more professionals or from misplaced priorities.

Removing the prospects of skilled workers to advance their careers abroad might also undermine the incentive for people to invest in further education, which in turn could severely undermine the growth of human knowledge and skills. In addition, policies that would lock talented people in their countries of birth would violate the internationally accepted right of freedom of movement. These and other considerations led the World Bank to conclude in its *World Development Report*, "Going against the political tide . . . we argue that greater migration would be good for both equity and efficiency."

CONCLUSION: ANOTHER WAY TO LOOK AT POPULATION IN AFRICA

Conventional wisdom holds that Africa has more people than its material conditions (including fragile land and lack of water) can support, and that the continent's rapid population growth rate is a recipe for continued poverty and underdevelopment. According to this line of thinking, as more and more people compete for a slice of a small economic pie, the size of the slices becomes smaller and smaller.

For the most pessimistic of observers, Africa's plight represents the realization of a prediction made more than 200 years ago by the British economist Thomas Malthus. Population will grow much faster than a country's food supply, Malthus believed, unless checked by "moral restraints" such as war, disease, and famine. In the absence of international food aid, neo-Malthusians argue, great numbers of Africans will continue to face hunger and famine—and the continent will remain largely destitute—unless population growth can be brought under control through the implementation of family planning measures.

NOT ENOUGH PEOPLE?

Some economists have argued that the conventional wisdom regarding Africa and population is completely wrong. Africa, they assert, suffers not from overpopulation but from underpopulation. The reason, according to these economists, is that low population densities in much of the continent stifle the sort of development that would produce economic growth. In other words, insufficient numbers of people prevent the size of the pie from being increased.

One of the most prominent advocates of this view was the economist Peter Bauer. In his book *The Development Frontier* (1991), Bauer attacked the Malthusian view of population growth as a block on development in poor countries. On the contrary, he contended, sparseness of population has inhibited economic progress in much of the less developed world. "It retards the development of transport facilities and communications, and thus inhibits the movement of people and goods and the spread of new ideas and methods. These obstacles to enterprise and economic advance are particularly difficult to overcome," wrote Bauer.

A crucial point to keep in mind when considering the adequacy of public services in a country is that a government's ability to provide more facilities depends on its finances. If the inhabitants are not contributing enough in taxes, either because they are too few in number or they are numerous but too poor, the state cannot provide the necessary services, regardless of the level of want (leaving aside foreign aid). The point made by Bauer and other like-minded economists is that where a population is too small in size, there is likely to be insufficient demand for infrastructure services, such as roads, electricity, and communications, to warrant their supply. These services are not only measures of a good standard of living but also essential to future economic growth.

Residents of Kyelitsha, a poor South African township outside Cape Town, demand better living conditions, including electricity, clean drinking water, and sanitation. Where government budgets are strained—as they are in most African countries—decisions on whether or not to invest in infrastructure in a particular area often hinge on how many people live in that area. The less densely populated the place, the more difficult it is to justify costly projects.

When considering the relationship between population growth and poverty, it is useful to bear in mind that virtually nothing in life is free—so what appears to be a shortage of particular public goods or services may reflect either a lack of demand or the inability of providers to supply, rather than a population too large to provide for. In economics demand is the desire *and* ability to purchase a good or service, while supply refers to goods and services offered for sale at prices that at least cover the supplier's costs.

Even air and water are not free if what is supplied are clean air and safe water. These require costly measures to combat air pollution or to build pipes and purify water, paid for by the government (taxpayers) or industry (and hence the consumer). When government provides the poor with free health care, the service is not actually free because other people—taxpayers—foot the bill. So the availability of infrastructure and public services in a society depends on its ability to pay for them, rather than the number of inhabitants it has. Population growth increases want in a country, but it is demand (want plus ability to pay) and supply that determines whether the amount of resources available is adequate for the size of the population.

Low population density can be an obstacle to the provision of services to poor communities. For example, while it may be morally just for a government to build a road linking a remote, sparsely populated village to the national network, it may not be

This outdoor communal tap, near Turmi, Ethiopia, constitutes greater access to safe drinking water than hundreds of millions of Africans enjoy.

economically justifiable. This is because the opportunity cost of providing such a road is much higher than the likely benefit. Opportunity cost is the foregone alternative to any expenditure. In other words, the money used to construct a road to link a few dozen village families to the main highway could have been used to build a clinic elsewhere that would have served hundreds of people. In managing their limited resources, governments invariably must consider the cost in relation to the likely benefit and the alternative uses to which funds may be put.

In this regard, it often makes more sense to provide services for larger concentrations of people. The reality is that anywhere in the world, roads tend to be built to link high-density settlements or provide a means for transporting valuable commercial goods. This is because, like any other infrastructure and service, roads cost money, so users have to pay for it directly or indirectly.

Africa has a sparse road network, and where roads do exist they are typically in poor condition. This makes the movement of people and products slow and expensive, thereby impeding economic development.

In most sub-Saharan African nations, infrastructure is deficient. For example, these nations have very few roads, and most of the ones they do have are concentrated in a few cities and towns. For example the Netherlands (with a population of 16.6 million people and a surface area of about 16,000 square miles) has more than three times the road network as Ethiopia (with a population of 91 million and surface area of about 426,000 square miles). Furthermore, Africa's roads are often unpaved and in poor condition. Less than 19 percent of roads in sub-Saharan Africa are paved, the lowest level of all regions, according to the World Bank. South Africa has the biggest road network in Africa, but even its 225,000-mile road network is modest compared with that of the Netherlands, given that the African country is nearly 30 times bigger than the tiny European nation.

A similar story can be told with respect to electricity supplies. The majority of people in Africa are unconnected to national power grids. Electric power consumption in sub-Saharan Africa was 513 kilowatt hours (kwh) per capita, more than the 394 kwh per capita consumed in South Asia but substantially less than the 1,184 kwh used in the fast-growing East Asia and Pacific region, not to mention the more than 9,500 kwh consumed by high-income countries.

Comparisons between sub-Saharan Africa and other major regions of the world on virtually all other infrastructure services will show that Africans are on average less endowed than people in other places, except perhaps South Asia.

The primary responsibility for construction of infrastructure such as roads and bridges, national power grids, and water supply systems typically falls to government. Similarly, government usually plays a central role in the provision of education and health care. But other services essential to economic expansion and poverty reduction typically rely on private investment. And, as is the case with government-provided services, low population density may be an impediment to private investment in poor areas. That's because insufficient numbers of potential consumers make the prospect of gaining a return on investment very slim. For example, a commercial bank is unlikely to set up a branch in a remote village, since the volume of transactions is unlikely to provide sufficient revenue to make the venture worthwhile.

NEED FOR MORE CAPITAL INVESTMENT!

Aware of African countries' low levels of essential infrastructure, some development economists argue that the continent needs to accumulate more physical capital (human-produced physical assets that are capable of generating income, such as factories, machinery, and electricity grids) in order to reach a take-off point for industrial growth that will lift general living standards. For example, the World Bank says that, for Africa to reach an average GDP growth rate of 7 percent a year—necessary to achieve the Millennium Development Goal of halving poverty by 2015—annual investment of $20 billion in infrastructure will be required. That sum is about double what has been invested annually in the past. The World Bank said that about 40 percent of the investment in infrastructure should go into roads, and 20 percent each into energy and water. The World Bank and other donor and anti-poverty agencies believe that, because African nations are too poor to finance the investments by themselves, they require assistance from rich nations to help give them a big push.

The residents of this makeshift settlement in South Africa have illegally tapped into an electric power line. Most people in sub-Saharan Africa are not connected to national power grids.

But other economists question the idea that Africa's poor economic performance stems from having insufficient assets to propel rapid growth and poverty reduction. They also dispute the proposition that higher investment in physical capital by governments in Africa is the key to solving the region's development problems.

As a percentage of GDP, public investment—that is, government spending on infrastructure, education, health care, and so on—in Africa has been roughly the same as in other developing regions. What has been remarkable about public investment in many countries in Africa has been the dismal performance of state services and the low returns from the expenditures. This situation has led to the conclusion that the predicament facing African countries is not so much the lack of capital, but rather an inability to use the facilities they already possess. Under these circumstances, accumulating more capital would not by itself lead to faster growth or the eradication of poverty.

A good illustration of this point is Nigeria. Since the early 1970s Nigerian governments, mainly military regimes, have invested huge sums of money in building infrastructure, industries, and public services, yet Nigerians are as poor today as they were in the 1960s. Between 1965 and 2000 the country earned a total of $350 billion from oil sales, much of which was invested. There was rapid accumulation of physical capital, averaging nearly 7 percent a year. Between 1973, when world oil prices spiked because of strife in the Middle East, and 1980 Nigeria's stock of capital grew at an average rate of 14 percent, resulting in the tripling of capital stock in eight years. The government built all sorts of structures, including factories, highways, education establishments, and hospitals.

However, much of the physical capital was wasted through mismanagement and underutilization. An indication of the waste is the low level of capacity utilization (the actual level of output compared with the maximum level) in the manufacturing

Children at the Vukani Senior Primary School, in Qunu, South Africa, attend class in an old school bus. Despite substantial public investment, educational facilities—particularly at the postsecondary level—remain substandard in many areas of Africa.

sector, a substantial part of which was owned by the state. Whereas capacity utilization in manufacturing averaged about 77 percent in the mid-1970s, it plummeted to as low as 35 percent in the late 1990s (though it has recovered a little since the 1999 restoration of civilian government).

An often cited illustration of the gross waste of capital in Nigeria is the investment of as much as $8 billion in setting up a steel sector—a steel sector that has produced very little steel. The majority of the state-owned steel plants have been idle or producing at incredibly low rates for most of their existence. Since the 1970s nearly $5 billion was sunk into the white elephant Ajaokuta steel complex, which until its privatization in 2004 had not produced a commercial quantity of steel.

Nigerian governments also invested billions of dollars in electricity infrastructure, but the state power utility has operated well below its installed generation and distribution capacities, leading to frequent power outages that hurt households and businesses. Today the state power company is still struggling to produce at above 60 percent of its installed capacity of about 6,000 megawatts.

Virtually every capital investment by Nigerian governments has resulted in waste and underutilization. Economists Xavier Sala-i-Martin and Arvind Subramanian, in the 2003 International Monetary Fund report *Addressing the Natural Resource Curse: An Illustration from Nigeria*, observed that some two-thirds of the investment in manufacturing by the Nigerian government has been consistently wasted. "The overall picture that emerges is that Nigeria has invested in physical capital and has suffered from low productivity. Quality has suffered at the expense of quantity."

The reasons for the waste are complex, but the major underlying factors are plundering by corrupt rulers, especially under military dictatorships, and lack of the knowledge and skills necessary to use the capital productively. This suggests that the size or growth rate of Nigeria's population has had little direct bearing on the shortage of infrastructure and public services in the country. The electricity supply is not scarce primarily because too many people require the service in relation to available resources, but because the producers lack the ability to produce effectively.

Where there is a dearth of knowledge and human skills, and the environment is not conducive to high productivity, as is the case in much of Africa, merely increasing the ratio of capital to people—either by increasing the supply of capital or by contracting the population—will not by itself spur economic growth or reduce poverty. For example, making more computers available to a firm that lacks staff with relevant technological know-how will not increase its output. One computer with one talented operator could produce a software program that turns a struggling firm into a multimillion-dollar enterprise. By contrast, 100 similar computers with 100 incompetent operators would be a waste of capital.

FOSTERING INNOVATION AND ENTREPRENEURSHIP

In today's global economic climate, the capacity of countries to create decent jobs is linked to their international competitiveness. Though the world economy has been expanding strongly, there has been little growth in manufacturing jobs. For example, between 1995 and 2012 there was little change in the share of manufacturing in global employment. (It remains around 20 percent.) The main change has been a shift of jobs from agriculture to the services sector. This suggests that in coming years international competition for decent manufacturing jobs will get much tougher.

This is a matter of concern for African policy-makers who must figure out how new jobs will be created for the millions of young Africans who are either unemployed or underemployed. The proportion of Africa's working population in gainful

With equipment provided by the American charitable organization Africare, a woman in rural Mozambique makes soy milk in her home. Many development experts believe that encouraging entrepreneurship and increasing trade hold more promise for reducing poverty than does lowering population growth.

employment is relatively high compared to most other regions of the world. In 2012 employment-to-population ratio in sub-Saharan Africa was 63.9 percent, slightly down from 69 percent in 1995. The high percentage of the population in employment largely reflects the need of most African households to have as many as possible of their members earning incomes to contribute to the family's survival.

The big problem is that the vast majority of jobs being done are unskilled and generate little income. According to ILO estimates, the number of working poor—workers earning less than $1 a day—in sub-Saharan Africa was over 315 million in 2013. The region has the highest proportion of working poor in the world, although in absolute numbers there are more low earners in the South Asia region. The number of workers in sub-Saharan Africa earning $2 a day or less was 430 million in 2013.

Many economists expect to see little change over the next decade in the proportion of African workers on poverty pay. According to ILO projections, while the share of extreme working poor in other developing regions is liable to fall substantially by 2020 and the world average drop to 12 percent from 19.7 percent in 2003, more than 50 percent of the sub-Saharan Africa population is expected to be among the working poor in 2020.

In many ways the labor market situation in Africa is tied to conditions in the global labor market. African workers are competing for decent and productive employment with workers in other parts of the world. The challenge facing virtually all countries in the world is how to deal with international competition. Firms and nations have at least three ways to respond to competition: protectionism, price cutting, and innovation. Protectionism involves restricting entry to competitors. Price cutting entails lowering production costs to undercut the competition. Innovation is using new ways (technology) to combine factors of production to create a new or improved product for the market, thereby enjoying a monopoly, albeit temporarily.

According to economists, innovation is the main strategy being used by companies in developed nations, though some governments and firms still favor protectionism. Given that the cost of capital goods (plants and machinery) has become increasingly similar across nations, there is a limit to the extent that companies can compete by lowering their costs to undercut their competitors. In the case of companies in Africa, cost-matching competitors in Asia is particularly difficult because of Africa's low labor productivity (output per worker). Although labor productivity in Africa has improved since the mid-1990s, more progress has been made in this respect in Asia.

All this means that to prosper in the global economy, African nations must endeavor to become more innovative. Rather than simply trying to grow more of their old commodities like cocoa and cotton, or struggle to undercut Chinese garment makers, they must also seek to engage in new economic activities and use new methods to achieve old goals. This could, for instance, mean growing new varieties of crops, perhaps genetically modified crops; producing new styles of garments for local and global markets; and entering totally new enterprises.

Many economists who have sought to understand why some nations are wealthy and others are poor have concluded that the most important differentiating factor is people's knowledge and creativity, especially in using technology. From the time of the Industrial Revolution in Britain, the power of innovation is what has driven capitalism—and today this is even more the case.

The problem in most African countries is that people with entrepreneurial inclinations operate in a socio-political atmosphere that stifles creativity. Governments fail to adequately protect individual property rights, and unproductive elites use different means to extract unearned benefits from more productive citizens.

The challenge facing African nations is to establish a socio-political order in which individuals can be creative and innovation is appropriately rewarded. This will include measures to promote peace and stability, good governance, the rule of law,

A technician checks a machine at a cotton-processing factory in Bouake, Ivory Coast. To prosper in the global economy of the 21st century, African industries such as textile and garment manufacturing will have to be open to innovation.

sound economic policies, and quality education.

Without an environment that supports entrepreneurial activities, the majority of African nations will most likely continue to languish in poverty. But this will not be because they are overpopulated or because they are underpopulated but because their people lack economic freedom. Knowledge and freedom are the keys to economic growth and prosperity and are what neutralizes the pauperizing effect of rapid population growth envisaged by Malthusians.

Appendix

Algeria
Population: 38,087,812
Population Growth Rate: 1.92 %
Birth Rate: 24.4 births/1,000 population
Death Rate: 4.3 deaths/1,000 population
Life Expectancy: 74.73 years

Angola
Population: 18,565,269
Population Growth Rate: 2.78 %
Birth Rate: 39.36 births/1,000 population
Death Rate: 12.06 deaths/1,000 population
Life Expectancy: 54.59 years

Benin
Population: 9,877,292
Population Growth Rate: 2.88 %
Birth Rate: 37.55 births/1,000 population
Death Rate: 8.79 deaths/1,000 population
Life Expectancy: 60.26 years

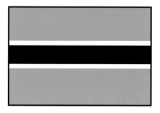

Botswana
Population: 2,127,825
Population Growth Rate: 1.48 %
Birth Rate: 22.02 births/1,000 population
Death Rate: 12 deaths/1,000 population
Life Expectancy: 55.74 years

Note: All figures are 2013 estimates.
Source: CIA World Factbook, 2013.

Burkina Faso

Population: 17,812,961
Population Growth Rate: 3.07%
Birth Rate: 43.2 births/1,000 population
Death Rate: 12.47 deaths/1,000 population
Life Expectancy: 54.07 years

Burundi

Population: 10,888,321
Population Growth Rate: 3.10%
Birth Rate: 40.58 births/1,000 population
Death Rate: 9.36 deaths/1,000 population
Life Expectancy: 59.24 years

Cameroon

Population: 20,549,221
Population Growth Rate: 2.08%
Birth Rate: 32.49 births/1,000 population
Death Rate: 11.66 deaths/1,000 population
Life Expectancy: 54.71 years

Cape Verde

Population: 531,046
Population Growth Rate: 1.43%
Birth Rate: 21.21 births/1,000 population
Death Rate: 6.28 deaths/1,000 population
Life Expectancy: 71 years

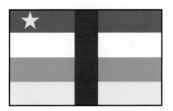

Central African Republic

Population: 5,166,510
Population Growth Rate: 2.14%
Birth Rate: 36.13 births/1,000 population
Death Rate: 14.71 deaths/1,000 population
Life Expectancy: 50.48 years

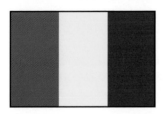

Chad

Population: 11,193,452
Population Growth Rate: 1.98%
Birth Rate: 38.7 births/1,000 population
Death Rate: 15.16 deaths/1,000 population
Life Expectancy: 48.69 years

Comoros
Population: 752,288
Population Growth Rate: 2.06%
Birth Rate: 31.49 births/1,000 population
Death Rate: 8.19 deaths/1,000 population
Life Expectancy: 62.74 years

D.R. Congo
Population: 75,507,308
Population Growth Rate: 2.58%
Birth Rate: 37.05 births/1,000 population
Death Rate: 10.8 deaths/1,000 population
Life Expectancy: 55.74 years

Republic of Congo
Population: 4,492,689
Population Growth Rate: 2.85%
Birth Rate: 40.09 births/1,000 population
Death Rate: 11.25 deaths/1,000 population
Life Expectancy: 55.27 years

Djibouti
Population: 792,198
Population Growth Rate: 2.29%
Birth Rate: 24.91 births/1,000 population
Death Rate: 8.08 deaths/1,000 population
Life Expectancy: 61.57 years

Egypt
Population: 85,294,388
Population Growth Rate: 1.92%
Birth Rate: 24.22 births/1,000 population
Death Rate: 4.8 deaths/1,000 population
Life Expectancy: 72.93 years

Equatorial Guinea
Population: 704,001
Population Growth Rate: 2.61%
Birth Rate: 34.88 births/1,000 population
Death Rate: 8.81 deaths/1,000 population
Life Expectancy: 62.75 years

Eritrea

Population: 6,233,682
Population Growth Rate: 2.42%
Birth Rate: 32.1 births/1,000 population
Death Rate: 7.92 deaths/1,000 population
Life Expectancy: 62.86 years

Ethiopia

Population: 93,877,025
Population Growth Rate: 2.9%
Birth Rate: 38.5 births/1,000 population
Death Rate: 9.3 deaths/1,000 population
Life Expectancy: 56.56 years

Gabon

Population: 1,640,286
Population Growth Rate: 1.977%
Birth Rate: 35 births/1,000 population
Death Rate: 13.07 deaths/1,000 population
Life Expectancy: 52.29 years

The Gambia

Population: 1,883,051
Population Growth Rate: 2.34%
Birth Rate: 33.41 births/1,000 population
Death Rate: 7.5 deaths/1,000 population
Life Expectancy: 63.82 years

Ghana

Population: 25,199,609
Population Growth Rate: 2.2%
Birth Rate: 32 births/1,000 population
Death Rate: 7.7 deaths/1,000 population
Life Expectancy: 61.45 years

Guinea

Population: 11,176,026
Population Growth Rate: 2.64%
Birth Rate: 36.6 births/1,000 population
Death Rate: 10.19 deaths/1,000 population
Life Expectancy: 58.61 years

Guinea-Bissau
Population: 1,660,870
Population Growth Rate: 1.97%
Birth Rate: 34.72 births/1,000 population
Death Rate: 15.01 deaths/1,000 population
Life Expectancy: 49.11 years

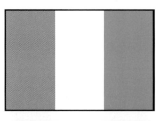

Ivory Coast
Population: 22,400,835
Population Growth Rate: 2.04%
Birth Rate: 30.4 births/1,000 population
Death Rate: 9.96 deaths/1,000 population
Life Expectancy: 57.25 years

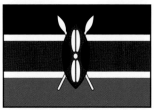

Kenya
Population: 44,037,656
Population Growth Rate: 2.44%
Birth Rate: 31.93 births/1,000 population
Death Rate: 7.26 deaths/1,000 population
Life Expectancy: 63.07 years

Lesotho
Population: 1,936,181
Population Growth Rate: 0.33%
Birth Rate: 26.65 births/1,000 population
Death Rate: 15.18 deaths/1,000 population
Life Expectancy: 51.86 years

Liberia
Population: 3,989,703
Population Growth Rate: 2.61%
Birth Rate: 36.45 births/1,000 population
Death Rate: 10.36 deaths/1,000 population
Life Expectancy: 57.41 years

Libya
Population: 6,002,347
Population Growth Rate: 2.01%
Birth Rate: 17.5 births/1,000 population
Death Rate: 4.9 deaths/1,000 population
Life Expectancy: 77.83 years

Madagascar
Population: 22,599,098
Population Growth Rate: 2.68%
Birth Rate: 34 births/1,000 population
Death Rate: 7.3 deaths/1,000 population
Life Expectancy: 64 years

Malawi
Population: 16,777,547
Population Growth Rate: 2.76%
Birth Rate: 40.42 births/1,000 population
Death Rate: 12.84 deaths/1,000 population
Life Expectancy: 52.31 years

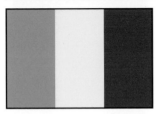

Mali
Population: 15,968,882
Population Growth Rate: 3.02%
Birth Rate: 46.6 births/1,000 population
Death Rate: 13.9 deaths/1,000 population
Life Expectancy: 53.06 years

Mauritania
Population: 3,437,610
Population Growth Rate: 2.32%
Birth Rate: 32.78 births/1,000 population
Death Rate: 8.66 deaths/1,000 population
Life Expectancy: 61.53 years

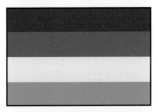

Mauritius
Population: 1,322,238
Population Growth Rate: 0.71%
Birth Rate: 13.78 births/1,000 population
Death Rate: 6.73 deaths/1,000 population
Life Expectancy: 74.71 years

Morocco
Population: 32,649,130
Population Growth Rate: 1.05%
Birth Rate: 18.97 births/1,000 population
Death Rate: 4.76 deaths/1,000 population
Life Expectancy: 76.11 years

Mozambique
Population: 24,096,669
Population Growth Rate: 2.44 %
Birth Rate: 39.34 births/1,000 population
Death Rate: 12.79 deaths/1,000 population
Life Expectancy: 52.02 years

Namibia
Population: 2,182,852
Population Growth Rate: 0.82 %
Birth Rate: 21.11 births/1,000 population
Death Rate: 13.09 deaths/1,000 population
Life Expectancy: 52.17 years

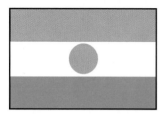

Niger
Population: 16,899,327
Population Growth Rate: 3.36 %
Birth Rate: 47.6 births/1,000 population
Death Rate: 13.4 deaths/1,000 population
Life Expectancy: 53.8 years

Nigeria
Population: 174,507,539
Population Growth Rate: 2.55 %
Birth Rate: 39.23 births/1,000 population
Death Rate: 13.48 deaths/1,000 population
Life Expectancy: 74.36 years

Rwanda
Population: 12,012,589
Population Growth Rate: 2.75 %
Birth Rate: 36.14 births/1,000 population
Death Rate: 9.64 deaths/1,000 population
Life Expectancy: 58.44 years

Sao Tome & Principe
Population: 186,817
Population Growth Rate: 1.99 %
Birth Rate: 37.02 births/1,000 population
Death Rate: 7.93 deaths/1,000 population
Life Expectancy: 63.49 years

Senegal
Population: 13,300,410
Population Growth Rate: 2.53%
Birth Rate: 36.19 births/1,000 population
Death Rate: 9.05 deaths/1,000 population
Life Expectancy: 60.18 years

Seychelles
Population: 90,846
Population Growth Rate: 0.92%
Birth Rate: 15.1 births/1,000 population
Death Rate: 6.9 deaths/1,000 population
Life Expectancy: 73.77 years

Sierra Leone
Population: 5,612,685
Population Growth Rate: 2.28%
Birth Rate: 38.12 births/1,000 population
Death Rate: 11.49 deaths/1,000 population
Life Expectancy: 56.55 years

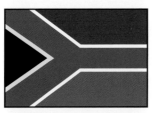

Somalia
Population: 8,863,338
Population Growth Rate: 2.85%
Birth Rate: 45.13 births/1,000 population
Death Rate: 16.63 deaths/1,000 population
Life Expectancy: 48.47 years

South Africa
Population: 48,601,098
Population Growth Rate: -0.41%
Birth Rate: 19.32 births/1,000 population
Death Rate: 17.23 deaths/1,000 population
Life Expectancy: 49.41 years

South Sudan
Population: 11,090,104
Population Growth Rate: 2.55%
Birth Rate: 34.53 births/1,000 population
Death Rate: 8.97 deaths/1,000 population
Life Expectancy: 58.92 years

Sudan
Population: 34,847,910
Population Growth Rate: 1.88 %
Birth Rate: 31.7 births/1,000 population
Death Rate: 8.3 deaths/1,000 population
Life Expectancy: 62.57 years

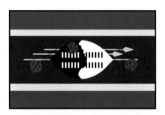

Swaziland
Population: 1,403,362
Population Growth Rate: 1.19 %
Birth Rate: 26.16 births/1,000 population
Death Rate: 14.21 deaths/1,000 population
Life Expectancy: 49.42 years

Tanzania
Population: 48,261,942
Population Growth Rate: 2.85 %
Birth Rate: 37.7 births/1,000 population
Death Rate: 8.6 deaths/1,000 population
Life Expectancy: 53.14 years

Togo
Population: 7,154,237
Population Growth Rate: 2.75 %
Birth Rate: 35.26 births/1,000 population
Death Rate: 7.78 deaths/1,000 population
Life Expectancy: 63.17 years

Tunisia
Population: 10,835,873
Population Growth Rate: 0.96 %
Birth Rate: 17.28 births/1,000 population
Death Rate: 5.87 deaths/1,000 population
Life Expectancy: 75.24 years

Uganda
Population: 34,758,809
Population Growth Rate: 3.3 %
Birth Rate: 45.8 births/1,000 population
Death Rate: 11.6 deaths/1,000 population
Life Expectancy: 53.45 years

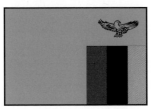

Zambia
Population: 14,222,233
Population Growth Rate: 2.89 %
Birth Rate: 43.1 births/1,000 population
Death Rate: 13.4 deaths/1,000 population
Life Expectancy: 52.57 years

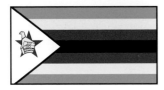

Zimbabwe
Population: 13,182,908
Population Growth Rate: 4.36 %
Birth Rate: 32.19 births/1,000 population
Death Rate: 12.38 deaths/1,000 population
Life Expectancy: 51.82 years

Glossary

CAPITAL—human-produced assets that are capable of generating income.

COLONIALISM—the control of the political affairs and resources of a country by another nation.

DEMOGRAPHY—the study of the characteristics of human populations.

ECONOMIC GROWTH—an increase in a country's capacity to produce goods and services, usually measured in terms of increase in per capita income.

FERTILITY—the average number of children a woman would have if fertility rates remain unchanged during her lifetime.

FRESHWATER—water that is not salty and is suitable for human consumption.

GROSS DOMESTIC PRODUCT (GDP)—the total value of goods and services produced in a country over a specific time period, usually one year.

INFRASTRUCTURE—the basic facilities and services needed for the smooth functioning of a country or area, such as transportation and communications systems, sewage and water installations, and other public utilities.

INVESTMENT—money or other resources put into property or other assets with the expectation of producing goods or services for future consumption.

MALTHUSIAN—pertaining to the doctrines of the British economist Thomas Malthus, especially the belief that population should be deliberately limited through the use of birth control.

MORTALITY—the ratio of deaths in an area to the population of the area.

PRODUCTIVITY—the relationship between output of goods and services and the input of resources (usually labor).

REPLACEMENT-LEVEL FERTILITY—the level of fertility needed to ensure that the size of a population remains stable over the long run.

UNDEREMPLOYMENT—a situation where workers work fewer hours than they want or in less suitable jobs than they are qualified for.

UNDERPOPULATION—a state of affairs in which the population is too small to optimally use available resources.

UNEMPLOYMENT—the existence of a section in the labor force that is able and willing to work, but is unable to find appropriate gainful employment.

URBAN AGGLOMERATION—a large city (or, in some cases, more than one city), along with its suburbs and highly settled contiguous areas.

Further Reading

Binns, Tony, Alan Dixon, and Etienne Nel. *Africa: Diversity and Development*. New York: Routledge, 2012.

Curtin, Phillip D. *The Atlantic Slave Trade*. London: A Census Publisher, 1969.

Lovejoy, Paul E. *Transformation in Slavery: A History of Slavery in Africa*, 2nd ed. Cambridge: Cambridge University Press, 1983.

Meredith, Martin. *The Fate of Africa: A History of the Continent Since Independence*. New York: Public Affairs, 2011.

Rotberg, Robert I. *Transformative Political Leadership: Making a Difference in the Developing World*. Chicago: University of Chicago Press, 2012.

Shillington, Kevin. *History of Africa*. New York: Palgrave Macmillan, 2012.

Williams, Paul D. *War and Conflict in Africa*. Malden, Mass.: Polity Press, 2011.

Internet Resources

HTTP://WWW.UNECA.ORG

The website of the Economic Commission for Africa, the regional arm of the UN in Africa, contains useful studies on different aspects of economic and social development in the continent.

HTTP://WWW.NEPAD.ORG

NEPAD, the New Partnership for Africa's Development, is "a vision and strategic framework for Africa's renewal." This website includes material reflecting the perspective of African leaders and governments on development and poverty reduction.

HTTP://WWW.WORLDBANK.ORG/AFR

The section of the World Bank site on Africa contains a wealth of statistics and analysis on a variety of topics related to development.

HTTP://WWW.UNFPA.ORG/PUBLIC

The website of the United Nations Population Fund, an international development agency, contains useful reports, especially relating to health.

HTTP://WWW.UNHABITAT.ORG

UN-HABITAT, the United Nations Human Settlement Programme, is mandated "to promote socially and environmentally sustainable towns and cities." Its website contains resources on urbanization in Africa and other regions of the world.

HTTP://WWW.WRI.ORG

The website of the World Resources Institute, an environmental think tank, provides a variety of useful information on the links between population and the environment.

HTTP://WWW.AFRICAECONOMICANALYSIS.ORG

Africa Economic Analysis is an independent online publication with articles on various economic and social issues in Africa.

HTTP://WWW.AFROBAROMETER.ORG

Contains reports on the attitudes of people in selected African countries toward different aspects of development.

HTTP://WWW.CSAE.OX.AC.UK

The website of the Centre for the Study of African Economies contains reports written by economists and social scientists studying African issues outside the continent itself.

Index

Numbers in **bold italic** refer to captions.

Opposite: Johannesburg is one of the largest cities in Africa, with more than 3.6 million residents.

This modest pump provides water to an entire African village.

Picture Credits

Contributors

PROFESSOR ROBERT I. ROTBERG currently holds the Fulbright Research Chair in Political Development at the Balsillie School of International Affairs in Waterloo, Canada. Prior to this, from 1999 to 2010 he served as director of the Program on Intrastate Conflict and Conflict Resolution at the Kennedy School, Harvard University. He is the author of a number of books and articles on Africa, including *Transformative Political Leadership: Making a Difference in the Developing World* (2012) and *"Worst of the Worst": Dealing with Repressive and Rogue Nations* (2007). Professor Rotberg is president emeritus of the World Peace Foundation.

DR. VICTOR OJAKOROTU is head of the Department of Politics and International Relations at North-West University in Mafikeng, South Africa. He earned his Ph.D. from the University of the Witwatersrand, Johannesburg, in 2007, and has published numerous articles on African politics and environmental issues. North-West University is one of the largest institutions of higher education in South Africa, with 64,000 students enrolled at three campuses.

TUNDE OBADINA, B.S., M.A., is a journalist and economist. He has worked for a number of organizations, including the British Broadcasting Corporation (BBC) and Reuters News agency. He is currently the director of Africa Business Information Service and is an external author for the Economist Intelligence Unit.